M000283675

HOW TO WRITE A DYNAMITE SCENE USING THE SNOWFLAKE METHOD

RANDY INGERMANSON

Ingermanson Communications, Inc.

CONTENTS

WANT TO WRITE A DYNAMITE NOVEL?

Do you want to write a dynamite novel?

I bet you do.

And I bet you can.

I'm here to teach you how.

Why do I think I can do that?

Because I've been teaching people how to write fiction for a long time.

I'm Randy Ingermanson, and writers all around the world know me as "the Snowflake Guy" in honor of my wildly popular "Snowflake Method" of designing a novel before you write it.

I've got a page on my website explaining the Snowflake Method. That page has been viewed more than six million times (as of January 2018). And I've published a best-selling book titled *How to Write a Novel Using the Snowflake Method.*

Tens of thousands of writers around the world are using the Snowflake Method right now to write their novels.

WHAT IS THE SNOWFLAKE METHOD?

The Snowflake Method is just a series of ten steps you can use to design your novel so you can get the first draft down on paper. People e-mail me all the time to say these steps work like magic to unlock their creativity.

Please note: the Snowflake Method doesn't make you more creative.

Because you already are creative.

The Snowflake Method just tells you *what task to be creative on next.*

You don't have to use all ten steps of the Snowflake Method. You can use any steps you like.

You can ignore any steps you don't like.

The ninth step in the Snowflake Method is to design each scene before you write it.

THE IMPORTANCE OF WRITING DYNAMITE SCENES

Why do scenes matter? Because the key to writing a dynamite *novel* is to write a dynamite *scene*.

When I first started writing fiction, my scenes just weren't working. Then I discovered Dwight Swain's classic book, *Techniques of the Selling Writer*. That book had a couple of chapters that changed my life. They taught me how to write a powerful scene.

If you can write one powerful scene, you can write a hundred. And that's a novel.

I've been teaching at writing conferences for many years, and I've critiqued manuscripts for hundreds of writers.

The #1 weakness I've found in beginning and intermediate writers is that *they don't write strong scenes.*

The absolute fastest way for most writers to take a quantum leap forward is to *learn how to design strong scenes.*

Dynamite scenes.

In this book, I'll teach you how. This is a short book, focused on just that one topic. You can blitz through it quickly and master scene design. You can.

As I said, I first learned how to design scenes from Dwight Swain's book, *Techniques of the Selling Writer*. I've now spent decades mulling his methods, rethinking everything, trying to simplify, and adding new ideas. This book is one result of those decades of work.

My one goal in writing this book is to teach you how to become an expert in designing powerful, amazing scenes that will move your readers' emotions.

Once you master *scenes*, you'll be one giant step closer to writing powerful, amazing *novels* that will move readers' emotions.

Let's do this, shall we?

Turn the page to get started.

Part One

STORY AND SCENE

Chapter One

WHAT YOUR READER MOST DESPERATELY WANTS

Your reader desperately wants one thing.

You have it in your power to give your reader that one thing.

And what is that one thing?

I could *tell* you what that one thing is, and you would nod and agree that yes, that one thing is clearly something all readers want.

But *telling* you that one thing wouldn't make it stick in your mind forever.

I want it to stick.

I'd rather *show* you that one thing. Once you've seen it, once you've lived it, you'll never forget it. That one thing will be inside you, fueling everything you write.

So let me tell you a quick story about one of our ancestors who lived many thousands of years ago in a small village on this planet we call home.

When I say he's our ancestor, I mean it literally—he's your ancestor and he's my ancestor and he's every human's ancestor.

That ancestor of ours was once a thirteen-year-old boy, the newest man in the village, and the smallest.

Imagine you're that boy on the day when word comes to the

village that there's a killer tiger ravaging the village's herd of goats.

THE TALE OF THE TIGER

You're furious. A drought has been burning the land for many months. That herd of goats is all that keeps your village from starvation.

You're also terrified. There's only one way to get rid of a killer tiger. The village has to organize a hunt, find the tiger, and kill it. But that won't be easy, because there's nothing more dangerous in your world than a killer tiger.

The village headman sends word around to the whole village. *All men meet in the village square, and bring your spear.*

When the messenger comes to your hut, he shakes his head and frowns. He thinks you're too young to go.

In your heart, you're afraid he's right. You only just became a man in the last month. You're small. You're skinny. You're weak.

But in your head, you know he's wrong.

If the village doesn't kill the tiger, it's going to steal every last goat, and the village is going to die.

To save your people, you and every man in the village have to work together to kill the tiger.

You know very well you might not come back. A thousand times in the village square, you've heard the village story-woman tell the Tale of the Tiger. You know that when a tiger is surrounded by men with spears, it always looks for the weakest man—and attacks that man.

Sometimes the man kills the tiger.

Sometimes the tiger kills the man.

You're terrified, but you know you have to go.

You grab your spear and run to the village square.

When you get there, the village headman smiles at you and shouts courage on you.

All the villagers smile at you and shout courage on you.

And then the men of the village set out to find the tiger.

You don't have to go far. You can hear the screams of a baby goat being dragged into the jungle. You can hear the roar of the tiger.

Every man of the village knows what he has to do. The Tale of the Tiger is in your blood.

You all fan out, forming a giant circle around the place where you heard the tiger.

The headman shouts the command to move, and you all advance ten paces.

He shouts again, and you advance ten paces.

Over and over and over again.

As you get closer to the tiger, the tightness in your chest squeezes your heart until the pain is unbearable.

The headman shouts, and you advance ten paces.

Sweat rains down your face.

The headman shouts, and you advance ten paces.

Your knees are shaking so hard, you think you're going to fall over.

The headman shouts, and you advance ten paces.

Finally, a war-shout goes up from all the men.

A hundred fingers point at a streak of orange and black, high up.

The tiger is in a tree, watching you with yellow eyes of rage.

He's trapped, fifty paces from where you stand. You can see him looking all around the circle, measuring his enemies. It's exactly like you imagined from every time you've ever heard the Tale of the Tiger. Exactly like it—only worse.

The headman shouts, and you advance ten paces.

The tiger roars—so loud you can feel the sound shaking your belly.

He's forty paces away. And he's looking directly at you.

The weakest and smallest man in the village.

Just like in the Tale of the Tiger.

The fate of the village is on your thin shoulders.

The headman shouts, and you advance ten paces.

The tiger screams with a terrible scream.

He leaps out of the tree.

He races straight at you.

Like you knew he would.

Time almost stops. In the last few instants before the tiger reaches you, you relive the thoughts of the hero of the Tale of the Tiger.

Always face the tiger. If you turn to run, you will die and so will the village. Face the tiger and kill or be killed. But face the tiger. Wait till the last possible moment before you throw. Then kill the tiger, even if the tiger also kills you. Face the tiger.

You want to run, but you face the tiger. You draw back your arm, clutching your spear in a sweaty grip.

The tiger lunges forward, straight at you, faster and faster, roaring in his fury.

Your body desperately wants to turn and run.

You face the tiger and wait for the perfect moment.

The tiger leaps in the air, and his roar is like thunder.

He reaches the peak of his flight.

He's coming down.

Straight at you.

You wait till the last possible moment.

You throw.

The tiger crashes into you, knocking you senseless.

Your very last thought before darkness falls is *I have done this before. I have done this a thousand times before.*

❄

W hen you come back awake, your head throbs and your whole body aches and all you can hear is the sound of drumming and dancing and feasting and shouting.

You're back in the village.

It's late at night.

The village is having a party.

The tiger is dead.

And you saved the village.

The whole village sees you're awake.

The village headman calls for silence.

All the village gathers around.

The village story-woman tells the Tale of the Tiger.

And you're the hero.

As the village story-woman tells the tale, you feel like you're living it all again. The great circle. The steady advances. The rush of the tiger. The blinding fear. The final leap. The desperate throw. The rage of the dying tiger.

And you're right. You are living it again.

But this is not the *second* time you're living the Tale of the Tiger.

It's the *thousandth* time you're living the Tale of the Tiger.

You lived it many times before, in story.

You lived it once today, in real life.

You're living it again now, in story.

And there's only a small difference between the story of the hunt and the real hunt. The real-life Tale of the Tiger was scarier, but not *much* scarier.

You were prepared for the real-life hunt by the thousand times you heard the Tale of the Tiger.

When the village story-woman finishes the Tale of the Tiger, a great shout goes up from all the village.

The village headman brings out the skin of the tiger you killed. He carries it to you.

He drapes it around your shoulders.

And all the people of the village take turns lifting you high in the air and shouting their thanks to you for killing the tiger.

And you realize that this is not the first skin you've worn today.

Every time you ever heard the Tale of the Tiger, you walked inside the skin of the hero of the Tale. You felt his fears. You faced his tiger. You killed his kill.

And today when you faced the tiger, you walked in that hero's skin again.

Yes, you killed the tiger.

But you had help.

The hero of the Tale of the Tiger also killed the tiger.

The village story-woman killed the tiger.

The Tale of the Tiger killed the tiger.

WHY STORY MATTERS

Our ancestors told stories about the things they feared most. Why? Because Story changes you. Story makes you strong. Story makes you brave. Story gives you hope. Story keeps you alive through the darkest night.

When you hear the Tale of the Tiger, it's almost as if you live in the hero's skin and face down his fears and kill the tiger.

Story builds emotional muscle memory.

When a real-life tiger comes your way, you have the emotional reserves to draw on.

Story teaches the tribe how to survive.

Story teaches the tribe how to thrive.

Story has been doing that for many thousand years.

Every human alive desperately needs Story.

Every human alive desperately wants Story.

Story is not a luxury item.

Story is not optional.

Story keeps the tribe alive.

WHAT STORY IS

Story is what happens when you walk through great danger in somebody else's skin.

And don't think that "great danger" always means a tiger.

There are other kinds of dangers, and other kinds of stories.

Romance is the best-selling category of story in modern fiction.

What is a romance novel? It's a story about a relationship going through great danger.

Danger so great, the relationship may very well be killed.

A romance novel builds in you the emotional muscle memory to keep your relationships alive.

Every kind of story builds a different kind of emotional muscle memory.

Story teaches the tribe how to survive, how to thrive.

Every kind of fiction you write will put your reader in the skin of some person going through great danger.

A POWERFUL EMOTIONAL EXPERIENCE

Facing danger is fun. There's probably some deep neurological reason why.

Certainly, facing danger makes you strong. Facing danger makes you bold.

But let's be honest here. Facing danger in real life is *dangerous*. You only get to make one mistake on a tiger hunt, ever.

Story is a safe way to face danger. Story teaches you how to face your fears, how to persist, how to hope when there is no hope. When you've got nothing else, Story will get you through. Story teaches you how to live.

And Story does all that by going deep into your neurons. Story teaches you how to live *by letting you live someone else's life.* You see what they see. You feel what they feel. You do what they do.

The reason Story goes deep is because it gives you a powerful emotional experience.

That powerful emotional experience is what creates in you the emotional muscle memory you need to survive and to thrive. In the heat of the hunt, when the tiger is racing at you, you'll forget everything you were ever *told.*

But you won't forget the things you already *lived.*

Story is like chocolate broccoli. It tastes incredibly great *and* it's amazingly good for you.

That's why you desperately need Story.

That's why your reader desperately needs Story.

That's why your main goal as a fiction writer is to give your reader the one thing she most desperately needs.

Story.

WHAT THIS BOOK IS ABOUT

The **Advanced Fiction Writing** series of books is all about how to write stories that give your reader a powerful emotional experience.

This book teaches you one important tool for doing that— writing a dynamite scene. Every scene in your story needs to move your reader's emotions. You can't afford to have any scenes that don't.

But before we focus on scenes, we have to ask a very important question.

How does Story create a powerful emotional experience? How exactly does it work?

The answer is simple. Story has two essential parts. Only two.

Turn the page to find out what they are.

Chapter Two

A STORY IS A CHARACTER IN A CRUCIBLE

How does Story create a powerful emotional experience? By putting a Character in a Crucible.

A Character is somebody your reader can relate to. At the beginning of the story, your reader steps inside the Character's skin. During the story, your reader feels like she is the Character.

Your reader sees what your Character sees.

Your reader hears what your Character hears.

Your reader feels what your Character feels.

That could be really boring, if you showed all the everyday parts of your Character's life.

But Story is not boring because *it only shows your Character in a Crucible*. And a Crucible is never boring. A Crucible is terrifying.

A Character in a Crucible can't help but feel a rush of emotions.

And your reader feels those emotions right along with your Character.

Those emotions lock that experience tight into your reader's neurons.

So Story needs exactly those two parts, a Character and a Crucible.

Without a Character, you don't have a Story.

Without a Crucible, you don't have a Story.

WHAT'S A CHARACTER?

A Character is a person who wants something desperately. She wants one of these three things:

- To *have* something.
- To *be* something.
- To *do* something.

That *something* is her Story Goal, and as your novel progresses, your Character comes to understand better and better what she wants, and to pursue it harder and harder. In this book, we're going to look at three examples from major novels that I've found helpful in my teaching over the years. We'll dive deep into these examples as we move through the book.

To start with, let's look at the Character in each example.

Example 1: Katniss Everdeen in *The Hunger Games*, by Suzanne Collins

Katniss is a sixteen-year-old girl who lives in a futuristic dystopian America in which the wealthy Capitol holds all the outlying districts in poverty. Katniss and her family live just on the edge of starvation, and all Katniss wants is to survive. When Katniss's younger sister's name is drawn to participate in the Hunger Games, Katniss volunteers to take her place. She'll be put in an arena with twenty-three other teens. They'll fight to the death, and the last one standing gets to live. Katniss desperately wants to live.

Example 2: Claire Randall in *Outlander*, by Diana Gabaldon

Claire Randall is a young nurse in 1946 England. The war has just ended and she's getting to know her husband again on a vacation in Scotland. She accidentally steps through a time portal in an ancient stone circle and finds herself trapped in 1743, in the hands of the suspicious local Scottish laird, who wants to know who she is and where she came from. Claire can't possibly tell him she's a time traveler. All she wants is to get back to the stone circle and return to 1946.

Example 3: Michael Corleone in *The Godfather*, by Mario Puzo

It's 1945, and Michael Corleone is the youngest son of a Mafia godfather, Don Vito Corleone. A few years ago, against his father's wishes, Michael volunteered for the Marines and fought bravely until he was wounded and released from service. Now Michael is in college. He wants to finish his education, marry his girlfriend, Kay, and get an honest job. More than anything, he wants to escape the criminal family he grew up in.

WHAT'S A CRUCIBLE?

A Crucible is the reason your Character can't have what she wants. The Crucible is partly the story world and partly the cast of other characters and partly what's inside your Character.

Your reader can relate to your Character because your reader doesn't get everything she wants either. Your reader may not want exactly the same thing your Character wants, but your reader knows what it is to desperately want something she can't have.

Your reader is in her own Crucible, and reading about your Character makes your reader's life more bearable.

Your Character's Crucible prevents her from getting or being or doing the one thing she believes would make her happy. The Crucible is what makes your Character miserable, and it's what makes your story worth reading.

Now let's have a look at the Crucible in each of our examples.

Example 1: The Crucible in *The Hunger Games*

Katniss just wants to live. What's preventing her? Twenty-two of the other teens in the arena are desperate to kill her so they can live. Some of them have been training all their lives to fight in the Hunger Games, hoping to win fame, wealth, and glory. These "Career Tributes" are powerful, fast, and lethal. The arena is well stocked with weapons. Cameras are everywhere, televising the games to a bloodthirsty public. The Gamemakers have complete control of the environment and can force the kids together where they'll have to fight each other. But one of the other teens doesn't want to kill Katniss. Peeta Mellark comes from Katniss's home district. He's been in love with Katniss since the age of five. Peeta doesn't want to kill Katniss. He wants to kill her enemies so she can live. But Katniss doesn't believe anyone could be such a fool, and she thinks Peeta's her worst enemy. Can Katniss teach her own cynical heart to trust Peeta—before the other tributes slice her to bits?

Example 2: The Crucible in *Outlander*

Claire Randall just wants to return to her own time. What's preventing her? First, she's held captive by the local laird, Colum MacKenzie, who thinks she may be an English spy or a French spy, or worse. Claire is an Englishwoman, and she was caught prowling around with no good explanation. Clearly, she's up to no good. But Claire has a worse enemy than Colum. Not far away in Fort William, there's an evil English army captain named Jack Randall, who just happens to be a distant ancestor of Claire's husband, Frank. Jack Randall is a vicious sadist, and he has his reasons for hating Claire. Claire has one real friend—a young Scottish outlaw named Jamie Fraser. Jamie is tall, handsome, and robust, and he's got a crush on Claire. Six weeks after Claire arrives in 1743, she's forced to marry Jamie. It doesn't take long before Claire finds herself returning Jamie's love. And it's an amazing love. There's an extraordinary soul connection between Claire and Jamie that she never had with Frank. But she did marry Frank first, and that means something to her. Can Claire find a way back to the time portal so she can return to Frank—and more importantly, can she leave Jamie?

Example 3: The Crucible in *The Godfather*

Michael Corleone just wants to live a decent, honest life. What's preventing him? His father, Vito Corleone, has recently turned down a lucrative deal offered by Virgil "Turk" Sollozzo, a heroin smuggler backed by one of the rival Families in the New York underworld. Sollozzo orders a hit on Vito Corleone, and it nearly succeeds. Vito is barely alive and unable to make decisions, while his battered Family enters an all-out war with Sollozzo and the Tattaglia Family. The odds are long against the Corleones. Michael has two older brothers, but neither is a good leader. The Corleone Family has plenty of foot soldiers, but they need to knock out Sollozzo if they want any hope of staying alive. Michael agrees to kill Sollozzo—but this sucks him into the criminal world he detests. And now he's on the run, because in killing Sollozzo, he's also killed a captain in the New York Police Department. Can Michael find peace and safety in this life, ever again? And what's to become of his girlfriend, Kay, who comes from a decent, honest, hardworking family like the one Michael always wanted? Will Michael become the one thing he most desperately doesn't want to be—the new Godfather?

HOW STORIES CREATE POWERFUL EMOTIONAL EXPERIENCES

Your story tells what your Character does to break out of her Crucible. Your Character is going to fight and fight and fight. Not necessarily physically. Most of the fights will be emotional or mental. Your Character may lose a lot of fights, but the only one that matters is the last one. There are three ways this can end:

- If your Character wins in the end, that's one kind of powerful emotional experience, a *happy ending*.
- If the Crucible wins in the end, that's another kind of powerful emotional experience, a *sad ending*.
- If your Character and the Crucible split the win, that's a third kind of powerful emotional experience, a *bittersweet ending*.

Those are the three main options for your story as a whole. That's how you deliver a powerful emotional experience for your main story.

But it's not enough to do that just once at the end of your story. A story can be very long. Your reader isn't reading for just one powerful emotional experience at the end of your tale.

Your reader is reading for a whole string of powerful emotional experiences, over and over and over again.

Your job is to deliver those powerful emotional experiences, as many as possible.

You do that by breaking up your story into a long string of scenes. And by making every single scene in your story *a dynamite scene that delivers the goods*.

There's a simple secret to make sure every scene packs a powerful punch.

We'll find out that secret in the next chapter.

Chapter Three

EVERY SCENE IS A MINIATURE STORY

W e just saw that you need to give your reader a powerful emotional experience in every scene.

But how do you do that? What's the secret?

The secret is simple. You have to make sure that *every scene is a miniature story.*

Let's be clear what we're saying here. We already know that a story is made up of a long string of scenes.

The crucial point is that each of these scenes is its own miniature story, complete with a beginning, a middle, and an end that delivers a powerful emotional experience.

A scene is a story within a story.

That's the secret to making sure that every scene gives the reader a powerful emotional experience.

The logic is simple. Every *scene* is a miniature *story.* Every *story* gives a powerful emotional experience. Therefore, every *scene* will give a powerful emotional experience.

This may seem obvious, but go to any critique group and look at the scenes that writers bring to be critiqued. You'll be astonished how often they bring a scene that isn't a story in its own right. Maybe it fills in some backstory. Maybe it develops one of the characters. Maybe it just kind of wanders. All too often, it's not even close to being a story.

If a scene isn't a story, all on its own, then it's a bad scene.

Make that your mantra and you'll see an instant jump in the quality of your writing.

Every scene is a miniature story.

Every scene.

EVERY SCENE NEEDS A CHARACTER IN A CRUCIBLE

If every scene is a miniature story, and every story shows a Character in a Crucible, then every scene needs a Character in a miniature Crucible.

Let's be clear on this. You have a main story you're writing and it has a main Character in a main Crucible.

But that main story is composed of a number of scenes, each one a miniature story. So each scene puts one of your Characters into a miniature Scene Crucible that will last only until the end of the scene. That Scene Crucible is nowhere near as big and demanding as the main Story Crucible. The Story Crucible will last for the length of the main story. The Scene Crucible will last only until the end of the scene.

With every scene you ever write, or every scene you ever edit, ask yourself immediately,

- Who's my Character for this scene?
- What's the Crucible for this scene?

Those two questions are gold.

The rest of this book will work out the details. Right now, let's look at some example scenes from the example stories we looked at in the last chapter.

Example 1: A Scene in *The Hunger Games*

Before the Games begin, Katniss and the other tributes spend several days in training. Now it's time for each tribute to have a private session with the Gamemakers to show off his or her special skills. The Gamemakers will give each tribute a rating that may help them get sponsors during the Games. Katniss is determined to make a good showing and is delighted to find some bows and arrows. She's spent years hunting for her food, so archery is her superpower. But these bows are different from the one she has at home, and she misses her first couple of shots. By the time she gets used to the new equipment, the Gamemakers have stopped paying attention. They're crowded around the buffet table, where there's a gigantic roast pig. Katniss is furious. She's not big or strong or fast, but she has this one remarkable skill to show off and they can't be bothered to watch? In a blind rage, Katniss puts an arrow on the string, pulls it back, and shoots straight at the Gamemakers. The Gamemakers scream and scatter. When they come up for air, they see that Katniss has put her arrow right through the apple in the pig's mouth.

In this scene, the Character is Katniss.

The Crucible has several parts to it:

- Katniss has only a few minutes to impress the Gamemakers and possibly give herself a bit of an edge.
- The equipment is unfamiliar, and she blows her first chance to make a good impression.
- By the time she's got things figured out, the Gamemakers just don't seem to care.

Example 2: A Scene in *Outlander*

Claire Randall has just stepped through some stones in a standing circle and had a weird experience she doesn't understand. She's very disoriented and wanders down the hill to the plain below. There she sees a half-dozen Scotsmen having some

sort of battle with some red-coated soldiers. She assumes she's
wandered into a movie and backs into the woods, where she's
grabbed by a man who looks exactly like her husband. Only he
isn't. He says his name is Captain Jonathan Randall, and he
demands to know who she is. She tries to escape, but he's too
quick and strong for her. And he seems to think she's a prostitute,
based on the way she's dressed. Which is weird, because she's
dressed in normal clothes. Captain Randall interrogates her hard,
but she can't give a good explanation of who she is or what she's
doing here, and she can't escape. Claire is terrified. Will he kill
her? Rape her? Claire is rescued by a small, wiry Scotsman who
knocks out Captain Randall and drags her away into the bushes,
pulling her to the ground. She bites his hand, and then something
smashes her in the head, knocking her out cold.

In this scene, the Character is Claire.

Her Crucible has several parts:

- She's in 1743 and doesn't know it yet.
- She's captured almost immediately by the evil Captain
  Randall, who's in the middle of a skirmish with some
  local Scottish outlaws.
- She is dressed in a thin modern dress, which makes her
  look like a floozy by the standards of 1743.
- She has no good explanation for why she is here, and
  Captain Randall suspects her of being a spy.

Example 3: A Scene in *The Godfather*

Michael Corleone's father, Vito, was shot just a few days ago,
and now Michael's whole life has gone nuts. His family is on high
alert. They're talking about vengeance. And they're worried about
what their enemy Sollozzo will do next. They're also treating
Michael like he's an outsider, a civilian in a war zone. Which he is.
Michael's father lies sedated in a heavily guarded hospital room in

the city. Two armed police detectives are right outside his hospital room. Dozens of the Family foot soldiers are stationed in the Godfather's room, the hospital lobby, and the street outside. Late at night, after visiting hours are over, Michael takes a taxi to the hospital to visit his father. He's aghast to find none of the Family soldiers in the street. None in the lobby. None on the Godfather's floor. None in his room. And the police detectives are gone. The Godfather is completely defenseless. Michael learns from the nurse that everybody was cleared out just minutes ago. He sees immediately that another hit is coming, probably in the next few minutes. Michael calls his brother to send in reinforcements as fast as possible. He persuades the nurse to move his father to a new room. He tells his father to keep quiet, no matter what he hears. And then Michael walks downstairs and out onto the street to do whatever he can to prevent the hit men from finding his father. Michael is alone and unarmed. But at least the other side knows he's a civilian. Can he outwit them long enough for the Family foot soldiers to arrive?

In this scene, the Character is Michael.

His Crucible is as follows:

- His father is weak and sedated and can't be moved.
- All of the Family guards have been cleared away by the cops.
- The police detectives have also been called away.
- Another hit is coming within minutes, and there isn't time to wait for reinforcements to arrive.

BREAKING THE SCENE CRUCIBLE

Each scene in your story tells what one of your Characters does to break out of the Scene Crucible. Once the Character has broken out, that Scene Crucible is finished and the scene is over.

Then it's on to the next scene with a new Scene Crucible.

Some parts of the new Crucible may be the same as they were in the old. But at least one part of the old Crucible will be broken. At least one part of the new Crucible will be different.

Let's see how each of our Characters breaks their Scene Crucible in the examples we just looked at.

Example 1: How Katniss Breaks Her Scene Crucible

Katniss's Scene Crucible is her fifteen-minute private session with the Gamemakers, where she's been set up to make a bad impression. She breaks her Scene Crucible by shooting an arrow into the group of Gamemakers. She will never again be in the situation of trying to impress them. They're impressed! Her next Scene Crucible will be the result of the smashing impression she just made.

Example 2: How Claire Breaks Her Scene Crucible

Claire's Scene Crucible is her being held captive by Captain Randall. She is broken out of her Scene Crucible by the mysterious wiry Scotsman. Together, they escape the evil captain. Her next Scene Crucible will be her captivity by this Scotsman and his clansmen, who are just as suspicious of Claire as Captain Randall is.

Example 3: How Michael Breaks His Scene Crucible

Michael's Scene Crucible is that the killers are coming and they know where his father is. He breaks out of his Scene Crucible by hiding his father in a new room and calling his brother for reinforcements. Michael's next Scene Crucible will be outside on the street. Unarmed and alone, he'll be waiting for the killers to arrive, knowing that he has to hold them off for fifteen long minutes.

So at the end of the scene, you've broken the Scene Crucible and you'll never use it again. You're ready to move on to a new Scene Crucible.

But what about the Character? Do you need a new Character too?

There you have a choice. You can use the same Character in the next scene. Or you can bring in a different Character. You generally have only a few Characters in your story who are important enough to take the lead role in a Scene Crucible. Some novels have only one such Character. Some have several.

In the rest of this book, we'll focus on the details of either the Character or the Scene Crucible.

We'll start with the Character, because that's simpler.

You need to make three important decisions about your Character before you start writing your scene.

Read the next chapter to learn what those three decisions are.

Chapter Four

EVERY SCENE NEEDS A POINT-OF-VIEW CHARACTER

A scene is never emotionally neutral.

Suppose you're writing a scene about a bank robbery. That could be a really exciting scene, giving your reader a stupendously powerful emotional experience.

But there's a problem. *Whose* emotional experience will it be?

Your reader, obviously, will share this powerful emotional experience. But who will they share it with? To have that powerful emotional experience, your reader needs to *step inside the skin of one of the Characters*.

Will you put your reader inside the skin of the bank robber, who desperately needs money to pay for surgery for his mother who's dying of cancer?

Will you put your reader inside the skin of the aging security guard, who is three days away from retirement and dreams of long walks on the beach, away from the rat race?

Will you put your reader inside the skin of the teenage hostage, who came into the bank to open a new checking account and now has a bomb wired to her head?

WHOSE SKIN IS THE READER INSIDE?

So your first decision for your scene is to choose which Character to make your reader identify with. We could call this Character the "Scene Character," to highlight the fact that she's the Character in this particular Scene Crucible. But there are already three standard terms people use. The principal Character in a scene is commonly called the "point-of-view Character" or the "POV Character," or the "viewpoint Character." For consistency, we'll stick with the term "POV Character" throughout this book.

Your POV Character gives your reader an emotional yardstick.

The emotions your reader feels *will depend on who your POV Character is.*

Your story will have many characters, usually at least half a dozen, and often many more.

How do you choose which character should be your POV Character in this scene you're writing right now?

That's a tough question to answer.

You might be using only one POV Character for the entire story. In that case, there's no decision to make. Once you've settled on that one POV Character, they're it for every scene.

But most stories are written with more than one POV Character, and in that case, you have a choice.

A good rule of thumb is to ask who has the most to lose in each scene.

The person with the most to lose in a scene will probably have the most powerful emotional experience. That character is a good bet to be a strong POV Character. Remember that in every scene *you're giving your reader the emotional experience of your POV Character.*

Think about the Tale of the Tiger in chapter 1.

We could have used the village headman as the POV Character.

Or the village story-woman.

Or the mother or father of the young man who killed the tiger. Each of these might have made an interesting POV Character. But none of them stood to be killed by the tiger.

The character with the most to lose was the one the tiger singled out to attack.

That's why he's the POV Character.

So that's your first decision—who is your POV Character?

Once you've decided on that, you have to make another crucial decision.

You'd like to tell your story so vividly that *you create a movie in your reader's brain.* That means you must decide ...

WHERE DO YOU PUT THE CAMERA?

If you're making a movie, you have many choices on how you show each piece of the action. Here are a few of your options:

- You can put the camera on a character's shoulder looking out at the world, showing what that character sees.
- You can put the camera in front of a character, looking back at the character, focusing on the person himself.
- You can pull the camera back so it shows all the characters without really centering on any single one.
- Lots of other options.

But you're doing something even more complicated than making a movie. A movie only shows images and plays sounds. Your story shows images and plays sounds *and also tells the inner thoughts and feelings of your POV Characters.*

You have six basic strategies for doing all this. Each strategy is called a "viewpoint." Let's talk about each one and show an example.

Strategy 1: First-Person Viewpoint

In the first-person viewpoint, you narrate your story as if the POV Character is the author. You use the pronouns "I" and "me." You show the reader only the things the POV Character can see, hear, taste, touch, smell, or feel. You don't show anything the POV Character doesn't know.

Here's an example snippet, revising the Tale of the Tiger to be first person:

The tiger lunges forward, straight at me, faster and faster, roaring in his fury.

My body desperately wants to turn and run.

I face the tiger and wait for the perfect moment.

The tiger leaps in the air, and his roar is like thunder.

He reaches the peak of his flight.

He's coming down.

Straight at me.

I wait till the last possible moment.

I throw.

The tiger crashes into me, knocking me senseless.

My very last thought before darkness falls is *I have done this before. I have done this a thousand times before.*

Notice that in first-person viewpoint, you are putting the reader inside the POV Character's head, but not inside anyone else's. The reader knows exactly what the POV Character is thinking and feeling.

But the reader can only guess what the tiger is thinking, or the village headman, or the other characters, based on what the POV

Character can see of the tiger or the headman or the other characters.

The reader is *inside* the POV Character and *outside* all the other characters.

Strategy 2: Second-Person Viewpoint

In the second-person viewpoint, you narrate your story as if the POV Character is the reader. You use the pronoun "you." Again, you show only the things the POV Character knows.

Here's the same example from above, now in second-person:

The tiger lunges forward, straight at you, faster and faster, roaring in his fury.

Your body desperately wants to turn and run.

You face the tiger and wait for the perfect moment.

The tiger leaps in the air, and his roar is like thunder.

He reaches the peak of his flight.

He's coming down.

Straight at you.

You wait till the last possible moment.

You throw.

The tiger crashes into you, knocking you senseless.

Your very last thought before darkness falls is *I have done this before. I have done this a thousand times before.*

Notice that the only real difference between second person and first person is the choice of pronouns. In both cases, the reader is *inside* the POV Character and *outside* all the other characters.

Strategy 3: Third-Person Viewpoint

In the third-person viewpoint, you narrate your story as if the POV Character is neither the reader nor the author but some third person who can be known completely. Once again, you show only the things the POV Character knows.

But this time, you can't use the pronouns "I" or "you." In third-person viewpoint, you have to give the POV Character a name. (This is the reason I wrote the Tale of the Tiger in second person —because I don't have any idea what sort of names were used in the village.)

Let's show the same section from the Tale of the Tiger, this time in third person. Since I have to use a name for this viewpoint, I'll call our hero Yung.

The tiger lunges forward, straight at Yung, faster and faster, roaring in his fury.

Yung's body desperately wants to turn and run.

He faces the tiger and waits for the perfect moment.

The tiger leaps in the air, and his roar is like thunder.

He reaches the peak of his flight.

He's coming down.

Straight at Yung.

Yung waits till the last possible moment.

He throws.

The tiger crashes into Yung, knocking him senseless.

Yung's very last thought before darkness falls is *I have done this before. I have done this a thousand times before.*

Notice that in third person, we typically alternate between the POV Character's name and a pronoun. There are no hard rules on how you mix these up. You want to be clear. You want to avoid repetition.

Just as in first person and second person, the reader is *inside* the POV Character and *outside* all the other characters.

Strategy 4: Third-Person Objective Viewpoint

The third-person objective viewpoint is similar to the normal third-person viewpoint, but with two very important changes.

- In third-person objective, you see the POV Character from the outside, not from the inside. So you can see things he can't see, such as the spider dangling above his head.
- In third-person objective, you don't tell what the POV Character is thinking or feeling.

It's as if you were pointing a video camera at the POV Character and expecting the reader to figure out his thoughts and feelings from his words, his actions, and his facial expressions.

Third-person objective is hard. It forces you, the author, to think like an actor. In a movie, each actor has to show what he's thinking and feeling using his face, voice, and actions (unless the director decides to use a voice-over to tell the character's thoughts out loud, but this is not common in movies.)

Let's change the snippet from the Tale of the Tiger to try to show the hero's thoughts and feelings from the outside.

The tiger lunges forward, straight at Yung, faster and faster, roaring in his fury.

Yung's body twists as if to turn and run. But he doesn't.

He faces the tiger and waits for the perfect moment.

The tiger leaps in the air, and his roar is like thunder.

He reaches the peak of his flight.

He's coming down.

Straight at Yung.

Yung waits till the last possible moment.

He throws.

The tiger crashes into Yung, knocking him down.

Notice the changes we had to make. In the second sentence, we couldn't simply say what Yung wanted. We're outside Yung. So we had to show his body beginning to twist so he could flee. And then resisting that motion. This takes a little extra time.

In the very last paragraph, we couldn't tell what Yung was thinking, because we're not inside his head. So we had to remove the sentence of interior monologue. There's really no way to show that from outside Yung's head. So we've lost something by going to this viewpoint.

In third-person objective, the reader is *outside* all the characters, *including* the POV Character.

Strategy 5: Head-Hopping Viewpoint

The head-hopping viewpoint is a bit controversial. Many writers and editors believe this is not a valid viewpoint. But some think it's not only okay but a good thing. Personally, I'm not a fan, but I'd rather not lay down the law here, because there are people who like it.

So what is head-hopping? It's essentially an alternating form of third person in which you switch from one POV Character to another *within a single scene.*

People who dislike head-hopping argue that you are putting your reader inside the skin of multiple POV Characters in the same scene. Therefore, head-hopping is bad, because your reader doesn't know whom to root for.

People who like head-hopping argue that if you want to capture all the emotions in the scene, then you need to be able to get inside the heads of multiple characters. This is especially true in, for example, a scene from a romance novel in which *the relationship itself is the main character.* You can argue that the reader is rooting for the relationship, and a relationship takes two, and therefore it's legitimate to get inside two heads in one scene.

I won't tell you what to do. You can make up your own mind on this question.

Let's look at our example from the Tale of the Tiger. I'll hop heads midway through, going from Yung's mind into the mind of the old village headman, whom we'll call Auld. Since he had no role in this snippet before, I'll tweak things a little so that now he does.

The tiger lunges forward, straight at Yung, faster and faster, roaring in his fury.

Yung's body desperately wants to turn and run.

He faces the tiger and waits for the perfect moment.

The tiger leaps in the air, and his roar is like thunder.

He reaches the peak of his flight.

He's coming down.

Straight at Yung.

Yung waits till the last possible moment.

He throws.

The tiger crashes into Yung, knocking him flat.

The spear pokes out of the tiger's back. It has just missed

his heart. The great beast is still writhing, twisting, screaming in a death agony.

Auld races toward the tiger in giant strides that seem to take forever. He throws his spear into the tiger's heart.

The tiger collapses on top of Yung.

Auld heaves at the tiger's corpse, desperate to know Yung's fate. Is he too late? Could he have been quicker?

All that he can think as he rolls the tiger off the boy is *I have done this before. I have done this a thousand times before.*

We begin this snippet in Yung's head. We stay there until Yung throws his spear. Then we segue out of his head, pulling back the camera to show him knocked flat (rather than knocked senseless, which we can't know if we're not in his head). For a brief moment, we're in third-person objective. We're not in anybody's head. Then Auld comes on the scene. We show him running. We show him throwing the spear. And then we glide into his head and we know his thoughts. We've hopped heads.

In the head-hopping viewpoint, the reader is *inside* the POV Character and *outside* all the other characters; then the reader moves *outside* all the characters; then the reader moves *inside* a new POV Character while remaining *outside* all the other characters. It's a little bit like having two mini-scenes within a scene. And of course you can do that several times in a scene. But beware. The more you hop heads, the more you'll yank your reader around.

Strategy 6: Omniscient Viewpoint

The omniscient viewpoint is rarely used these days, although it was common in the nineteenth century. In the omniscient viewpoint, you give the reader a God's-eye view of the story. You might say that the POV Character is God. Of course, the God of the story is the author. So you could just as well say that the POV Character in omniscient viewpoint is the author.

In omniscient viewpoint, the reader can know what all the characters are thinking and feeling. In fact, the reader can know things none of the characters know. The reader can know the long history of the village, the current *zeitgeist* of the village, the whole future of the village. No character could know all that, but the reader can.

The omniscient viewpoint is hard to pull off, but it can be done.

The Tale of the Tiger was written to be up close and personal with one POV Character. In order to recast our snippet in omniscient form, we're going to need to pull back the camera and bring in more characters. We'll keep Yung and Auld, and we'll add in the other men of the village and we'll also get a look inside the tiger's head.

You can decide for yourself whether this is a good way to tell a story.

The tiger lunges forward, straight at Yung, faster and faster, roaring in his fury. He knows men are weak, and this small man is the weakest of the weak. He means to crush him like grass.

Like a hundred thousand men before him, Yung feels his body desperately wanting to turn and run.

Like a hundred thousand men before him, he faces the tiger and waits for the perfect moment.

Yung vaguely knows that a dozen men are racing toward him with spears. He does not know that none of them are near enough to help. The only man near enough is Auld, who is frozen into inaction, bewitched by the tiger's roar.

The boy will live or die, and nobody can save him but himself.

Too late, the men of the village shout, "Auld!"

Auld comes out of his trance. He draws back his spear and sprints.

The tiger leaps in the air, and his roar is like thunder.

He reaches the peak of his flight.

He opens his jaws, preparing to make a killing strike on the boy's neck.

Heart pounding, Yung waits till the last possible moment.

He waits.

He throws.

The spear enters the tiger's chest, missing his heart by a millimeter. The tiger is wounded but not killed. Shocked by this unforeseen agony, he loses focus on his prey, snapping his jaws shut on air. Blinded by pain, writhing, twisting, screaming, the tiger crashes onto the boy with five hundred pounds of primal fury.

Auld races toward the tiger in giant strides. Half a second too late, he throws his spear into the tiger's heart.

The tiger collapses in death, burying Yung.

Every man of the village sucks in his breath. Is the boy dead or alive?

Auld heaves at the tiger's corpse. He does not know it yet, but this seals his fate as village headman. In a month, there will be a new man, younger, stronger, bolder. Auld will be sent out to die. But in this moment, all he can think is that he has failed the boy, and how will he face the boy's mother and father?

The Tale of the Tiger has been lived a hundred thousand times, but it can have only two endings.

The hero lives.

Or the hero dies.

I n the omniscient viewpoint, the reader is outside all the characters, but all of them are perfectly transparent. The reader can know what all of them are thinking and feeling, but the reader can also know things that none of the characters can know. So omniscient viewpoint is not just head-hopping on a grand scale. It's bigger than that.

I've never been omniscient, but I bet it's harder than it looks.

So is using omniscient voice.

We've now covered two of the three questions you have to settle for each scene. You've chosen your POV Character. You've chosen your viewpoint. Now there's one final question.

WHEN DOES THIS SCENE HAPPEN?

You have three choices on how to locate your story in time, and they're pretty simple:

- Past tense
- Present tense
- Future tense

Past Tense

In past tense, you tell the story as if it happened in the past. This is the most common way fiction is written. Here's an example, written in third person:

Yung waited till the last possible moment.

He threw.

The tiger crashed into Yung, knocking him flat.

Present Tense

In present tense, you tell the story as if it's happening right now. This is becoming a bit more common than it used to be. Here's an example, again written in third person:

Yung waits till the last possible moment.

He throws.

The tiger crashes into Yung, knocking him flat.

Future Tense

In future tense, you tell the story as if it's something destined to happen in the future. This is rare, because it gives the feeling that the future is predestined, whereas we like to think we have choices. But you can imagine the village story-woman telling Yung how he is to behave if he ever faces the tiger, like this:

When the tiger begins his leap, you will long to throw your spear, but you will wait.

When the tiger reaches the peak of his flight, you will think it is too late, but still you will wait.

When the tiger is almost on you, when his shadow blots out the sun, when you are sure you cannot live, still you will wait.

You will wait and wait and wait until the last moment.

When you know that you know that you know that you cannot miss, that is when you will throw.

You will throw with all your power, a straight line through the tiger's heart.

The tiger will crash down on you with a scream more terrible than you ever heard.

Then you will live or you will die, as the gods decide.

But you *will* kill the tiger.

You *will* save the village.

You *will* live forever in the Tale of the Tiger.

IS THAT ALL THERE IS TO A CHARACTER?

In this chapter, we've covered three essential decisions you have to make in every scene:

- Who is your POV Character?
- What is the viewpoint for your POV Character?
- What tense will you use to show that viewpoint?

You may be thinking that there is much more to be said about Character. What about motivations? What about personal values? What about backstory?

All of those are important things, and they deserve a whole book, or maybe more than one book. We discussed some of these issues in my book *How to Write a Novel Using the Snowflake Method.* And I plan to cover some of them in more detail in later books in the **Advanced Fiction Writing** series.

But in this book, we are keeping very focused on one central question:

How do we structure a scene to give our reader a powerful emotional experience?

We know that the answer is to put a POV Character into a Scene Crucible.

We now know just enough about POV Characters to do that effectively.

Notice that we can keep reusing our POV Characters over and

over in different scenes. But we'll need to come up with a new Scene Crucible in every scene. That makes the Scene Crucible quite a bit more complicated than the POV Character.

For the rest of this book, we're going to look at the Scene Crucible.

Let's get started.

Chapter Five

EVERY SCENE NEEDS A CRUCIBLE

I t's worth summarizing what we've said before.

A scene is a miniature story.

A story is an account of a Character in a Crucible.

Therefore a scene is an account of a POV Character in a Scene Crucible.

So there are two Crucibles that we need to constantly keep in mind:

- The Story Crucible
- The Scene Crucible

The Story Crucible is all the things that conspire to ruin your lead Character's life for the entire length of your story. The Story Crucible is big. It includes your story world, your lead Character's whole life history up to this moment, and the life histories of all the other characters in the story.

And that's a big danger to you as a writer.

You will be powerfully tempted to spend a lot of words explaining all the amazing things that make your Story Crucible so terrible for your lead Character.

RESIST THE URGE TO EXPLAIN YOUR STORY CRUCIBLE

Don't do it. Your reader wants to know *what's happening right here right now*. Not what happened yesterday or last year or a thousand years ago. Not what's happening in the next room or the next city or the next country. All of those may be important parts of your Story Crucible, but don't tell them.

Well then, how are you supposed to write your scene? If you can't explain what the problem is, how are you going to get anywhere?

The answer is simple. You have a Scene Crucible *that is ruining your POV Character's life right here and right now*. Feel free to explain that Scene Crucible in this current scene.

Don't tell more than you need.

Do tell as much as you need to ensure that this scene makes sense.

If your reader needs to know what year it is, what place it is, what the weather's like, then tell the reader. Work it right into the scene.

If your reader needs to know about some law that is causing your POV Character pain in this scene right now, then explain the law.

If your reader needs to know about the geographical situation your POV Character needs to deal with in this scene right now, then explain the geography.

If your reader needs to know about some terrible thing that happened in the POV Character's life that is causing him pain right now, then explain that terrible thing.

You may be wondering how you'll ever be able to explain all that wonderful backstory you worked up and that fantastic story world you created.

Don't worry, you'll get there.

Remember, the Scene Crucible is going to last for exactly one scene.

At the end of the scene, your POV Character will break out of the Scene Crucible. He'll probably get hurt breaking out, but the Scene Crucible will be destroyed. In the next scene, there'll be a new Scene Crucible.

Scene by scene, you'll show your reader a long sequence of Scene Crucibles that will add up in the reader's mind to the whole Story Crucible. At the end of the story, your reader will know everything she needs to know about the Story Crucible to understand the story.

And she'll always get that information just in time.

THE SHAPE OF A SCENE

Over the last few centuries, writers have found two emotively powerful shapes for a scene. Only two. Here they are:

- A Proactive Scene
- A Reactive Scene

The rest of this book will laser in on these two kinds of scene. We'll break them apart, learn exactly how they work, and study some examples. By the end of this book, you'll be an expert on scene structure.

But first let's get a quick overview of them.

What's a Proactive Scene?

A Proactive Scene is a scene in which a POV Character begins with a Goal, faces numerous obstacles that create Conflict, and ends (usually) in a Setback. Occasionally, a Proactive Scene ends in a Victory, but this is rare. We'll see later why you usually want to end with a Setback, and why you have to occasionally end in Victory.

In a nutshell, a Proactive Scene is

1. Goal
2. Conflict
3. Setback (or Victory)

What's a Reactive Scene?

A Reactive Scene is a recovery scene that follows a Proactive Scene. The POV Character begins with an emotional Reaction to the Setback from a previous scene. She considers numerous options in a Dilemma, and she ends with a Decision.

In a nutshell, a Reactive Scene is

1. Reaction
2. Dilemma
3. Decision

And for each of these kinds of scene, we have a Scene Crucible.

THE SHAPE OF A SCENE CRUCIBLE

Your scene happens in a dangerous place, at a dangerous time, in dangerous circumstances. If you don't have danger in your scene, then your scene is not pulling its weight and you need to fix it or kill it. Fixing it means adding in danger. Killing it means throwing it away.

The dangerous parts of the scene are what we mean by your Scene Crucible.

Let's look at the two types of scene. What's the danger in each?

The Danger in a Proactive Scene

In a Proactive Scene, your POV Character has a Goal that she desperately wants to achieve by the end of the scene.

The danger is that she might not achieve her Goal.

So the Scene Crucible in this case is everything that is blocking your POV Character from reaching her Goal. The story world. The other characters. The POV Character's own weaknesses. Everything that keeps her from reaching her Goal.

The Danger in a Reactive Scene

In a Reactive Scene, your POV Character is reeling from the shock of a Setback in some previous scene.

The danger is that she might give up and quit the story.

So the Scene Crucible in this case is everything that is pushing your POV Character to quit. Depression. Fear. Guilt. Other characters. Lack of options. Everything that says there is no way forward, no new Goal to push for in the next scene.

HOW YOU KNOW WHEN A SCENE IS BROKEN

A scene is broken when you can't say what its Scene Crucible is.

Remember, every scene must be a miniature story.

Every story is a Character in a Crucible.

If you have no Scene Crucible, then your scene is not a story, and therefore your scene is broken.

Later in this book, we'll look at exactly how you fix a broken scene. That can take a bit of work. But for right now, the important thing is *to know when a scene is broken.*

You can't fix it if you don't know it's broken.

You might want to think for a moment about the scene you're working on right now.

Who's the POV Character for that scene?

What's the Scene Crucible?

Is your scene working, or is it broken?

If it's working, then you have a good chance of delivering a powerful emotional experience, which is your main job as a storyteller.

In the next chapter, we'll look at how that works. How does a Proactive Scene deliver a powerful emotional experience? What's the psychology of it?

Part Two

PROACTIVE SCENES

Chapter Six

THE PSYCHOLOGY OF A PROACTIVE SCENE

In a Proactive Scene, you're going to be working with your reader's brain to create a powerful emotional experience in your reader. Each part of the Proactive Scene is designed to punch certain emotive buttons.

Remember, there are three parts to a Proactive Scene:

1. Goal
2. Conflict
3. Setback (usually) or Victory (occasionally)

Let's look at each of these to understand why they're essential.

WHY A PROACTIVE SCENE NEEDS A GOAL

All humans are in a real-life Crucible most of the time. That's just what life is—constant struggle. When you're in a Crucible, the easy way to deal with your troubles is to not deal with them. To curl up and ignore your fears. Or to numb the fears with chemicals. Or to run from the danger.

But most of us don't admire people who take the easy way out.

We admire people who face the danger. And more—they attack the danger.

We admire people who are proactive. We want to be proactive. We want to, but we often fail, because *the proactive way is the hard way.*

The proactive approach to the Crucible starts with making a Goal and then going all in to attack all obstacles.

When you give a likable POV Character a Goal for a Proactive Scene, you immediately punch several emotive buttons in your reader:

- "I admire that POV Character for tackling the danger head on. She's brave!"
- "I want to live inside that POV Character's skin for this scene and learn to face my own dangers."
- "I am rooting for that POV Character to reach her Goal. Because I like her."

When you give an unlikable POV Character a Goal for a Proactive Scene, you punch several different emotive buttons:

- "I dislike that POV Character for tackling danger this way, or for creating danger for the person I like. She's awful!"
- "I'm going to live inside that POV Character's skin for this scene and learn how *not* to live my life."
- "I'm rooting against that POV Character. I want her to fail. Because I hate her."

WHY A PROACTIVE SCENE NEEDS CONFLICT

Conflict means resistance to your POV Character's quest to achieve his Goal. Every human faces Conflict in their life. Good things don't come easy. If you want to achieve a Goal, you have to work for it. You have to get creative. You have to stay strong, and keep on staying strong.

In short, you need to develop emotional muscle. And that's what Story does. It builds emotional muscle. And it creates emotional muscle memory. Those are two different things. Muscle is *the strength to do the right thing*. Muscle memory is *the ingrained ability to remember what the right thing is*.

Muscle builds up when it faces resistance.

When you make a likable POV Character face Conflict in a Proactive Scene, you immediately punch several emotive buttons in your reader:

- "I'm afraid for that POV Character. She's going into danger. She might fail."
- "I admire that POV Character for persisting through this long Conflict. She doesn't quit! Neither will I."
- "My heart rate is up and I feel alive in this moment. This is great!"

When you make an unlikable POV Character face Conflict in a Proactive Scene, you punch a somewhat different mix of emotive buttons:

- "I'm afraid that POV Character is going to succeed and make things even worse for a person I like. I can't bear to watch, but I can't bear not to. She might succeed!"
- "I resent that POV Character for persisting in creating Conflict for a person I like. She's not quitting, but neither is the person I like."
- "My heart rate is up and I feel alive in this moment. This is great!"

WHY A PROACTIVE SCENE USUALLY NEEDS A SETBACK

A scene is a miniature story. That means it needs to come to an end—with a resolution. The resolution can be a win, or it can be a loss.

When it's a loss for a likable POV Character or a win for an unlikable POV Character, we call that a Setback.

Setbacks are good. Your goal is to build emotional muscle memory in your reader. And I'm told that muscle builds up quickest when you exercise it to the point of failure.

When you end with a Setback in a Proactive Scene, you immediately punch these emotive buttons in your reader:

- "Ouch, that hurts!"
- "I can't believe that's the end of the scene. I hope that's not the end of the larger story. Please, oh please, oh please, let there be more to this story."
- "I must turn the page to see what happens next."

When you end a scene with a Setback, it's clear that the scene has ended, but it feels like the story as a whole has unfinished business. That creates an open loop in your reader's brain.

And human brains are not wired to accept open loops.

Human brains want closure.

Human brains insist on looking for closure.

Your reader *has to turn the page to get closure*. And that's what you want her to do. You want her to turn the page and read the next scene and the next and the next.

So when you end a scene with a Setback, you're exploiting the so-called "Zeigarnik effect"—the heightened focus that all humans have when they face an open loop. (The Zeigarnik effect is named for Bluma Zeigarnik, a psychologist who published her results in 1927. The story goes that her PhD adviser noticed in a restaurant that a certain waiter could remember tremendous detail about an order—until it was paid, at which point he seemed to forget everything. The payment closed a mental loop, and he lost focus.)

WHY A PROACTIVE SCENE SOMETIMES NEEDS A VICTORY

When a scene ends in a win for a likable POV Character or a loss for an unlikable POV Character, we call that a Victory.

As we just saw, a Setback punches some powerful emotive buttons. A Victory also punches some buttons:

- "Yay, that feels good!"
- "Now I can relax. Actually, what time is it? Uh-oh! I had no idea it was so late."
- "I don't really have to turn the page right now. Things are good. If I turn the page, things might go south, and I'd like to end my reading for today on a high note."

One of my friends once explained why she didn't want to enter any more writing contests: "It hurts more to lose than it feels good to win."

It's just a fact. Winning feels good. But losing feels *terrible*.

If your goal is to keep delivering a powerful emotional experience and to keep your reader flipping pages, you should deliver far more Setbacks than Victories.

But sometimes you have to end a scene with a Victory.

Because it's just not plausible that anyone would always always *always* lose.

And sometimes, the only way to lose is to die, which means your POV Character probably needs to live, which means she needs a Victory.

But even if you deliver a win at the end of your scene, you may still be able to turn that win to ashes if you're lucky. Then it becomes a bittersweet ending to a scene, and it has all the advantages of a Setback along with all the advantages of a Victory. More on that in a later chapter.

ADVICE ON GOALS, CONFLICTS, AND SETBACKS

Establish the POV Character's Goal as quickly as possible, preferably in the first sentence of the scene. Why? Because until you have a Goal, you have no story. The instant your scene gets a Goal, it becomes a miniature story.

Spend most of the scene in Conflict, with your POV Character trying and trying and trying to achieve her Goal. During the Conflict phase, your POV Character is neither succeeding nor failing. She's trying things with a Goal in mind, and she knows that she only has to find one thing that works in order to win. So she tries and tries and tries again.

At the end of most Proactive Scenes, give your POV Character a terrible Setback instead of her Goal. This is not just one more attempt that doesn't work. This is the *last* attempt. And not only does it not work, *it smacks your POV Character down hard*. It leaves your POV Character worse off at the end of the scene than she was at the beginning.

So now we understand the theory of how a Proactive Scene works.

But how do we make it work in practice?

We're going to break it down into parts and look at each part in detail.

In the next chapter, we'll explain exactly how you create a Goal that will drive your POV Character for a full scene.

Chapter Seven

HOW TO CREATE A DYNAMITE GOAL

L et's do a quick review.

Every scene in your story needs to be its own miniature story, complete with a beginning, a middle, and an end.

You begin a Proactive Scene by identifying the POV Character and making clear what his Goal is for the scene. That raises two questions.

- When do you identify the POV Character?
- How long should you take to establish his Goal?

Normally you should try to identify the POV Character in the first sentence, or at least the first paragraph. Once in a while, you might not do that, but you should have a reason for violating the norm.

There's no set answer on how long you should take to define the Goal, but try to do it as early as possible. If you can do it in the first sentence, that's excellent. If it takes a whole paragraph to make that Goal clear to the reader, that's still very good. The longer it takes to make the Goal clear, the less proactive the POV Character seems.

If it takes a lot longer than one paragraph, ask yourself why it's taking so much time. What's the holdup? What would happen if you moved things around so you got that Goal right up in the first paragraph or even the first sentence?

If you can improve your scene by moving the Goal earlier in the scene, that's a win. Do it.

But there's a larger question to ask.

How do you know that the Goal for this scene is a good Goal?

HOW DO YOU KNOW WHEN A GOAL IS GOOD?

A Proactive Scene is going to run anywhere from a few hundred words to a few thousand. In that scene, you have to tell a complete, self-contained story. So your Goal has some requirements.

A Goal Must Fit the Scene's Time Slot

The Goal for your Proactive Scene must be something that could reasonably be achieved in the time you've allocated for the scene. And normally a scene runs for a few minutes up to a few hours in story world time.

That's enough time to run a race. Or rob a bank. Or ask that special someone to marry you.

It's not enough time to train for the Olympics. Or corner the market on silver. Or organize a wedding. It'll take a large number of scenes to reach those Goals—maybe a whole novel.

So make sure the Goal fits the time available. If it doesn't fit, then break it down into a string of smaller steps, and use the first of these as the Goal of your scene.

A Goal Must Be Possible for Your POV Character

The Goal for your Proactive Scene must be something that your POV Character could conceivably do.

If your Character is slow, then it's silly to give him the Goal of breaking the world record in the marathon. That's just not physically possible.

If he's a fussbudget about obeying the law, then giving him the Goal of robbing a bank is going to make a very implausible scene, and you're going to have to work hard to get your reader to believe it's possible.

If he's terminally shy, then does that mean you can't give him the Goal of asking his secret crush to the prom? No! As long as he's physically capable of getting the words out, that is actually a fine Goal for a scene. The reason is simple.

A Goal Should Be Difficult

A story is about a Character in a Crucible. The tougher the Crucible, the more compelling the story.

So it's perfectly fine to make the Goal for your Proactive Scene difficult. In fact, it's good.

There's a fine line to draw here. The more difficult the Goal, the more tension, and that's good. But if the Goal is laughably difficult, then that's not believable. So give your POV Character a Goal that's hard, but not ridiculously hard.

And why would your POV Character choose such a difficult Goal? There's only one reason.

A Goal Must Fit the Character

Your POV Character has a certain set of Values. She has some Ambition that drives her life. And she has some major Story Goal for the larger story you're telling.

Your Character's Goal in the scene should fit in with these Values, this Ambition, and this Story Goal.

And what do we mean by Values, Ambition, and Story Goal? I covered those in depth in my book *How to Write a Novel Using the Snowflake Method*, but the short answer is this:

- **Values** are personal beliefs your Character holds that can be put like this: "Nothing is more important than _____." Whatever your Character writes in to the blank is a Value. Usually, your Character will have several Values, and they may conflict.
- An **Ambition** is an abstract thing that your Character wants to achieve in life. Miss America famously wants to achieve "world peace." But that's abstract. It looks different to different people.
- A **Story Goal** is the concrete, objective thing your Character wants to achieve in this story. It should ideally be something that could be photographed or videotaped. It is the thing that your Character believes would fulfill her Ambition. She might believe that eliminating all nuclear weapons would mean world peace has arrived. (Maybe it would and maybe it wouldn't, but that's what she believes. You can't photograph world peace, but you can photograph the elimination of the last nuclear weapon on earth.)

In each scene, your Character needs to set up a Goal that she believes is a stepping-stone on the way to achieving her Story Goal. It needs to be in line with her Ambition and her Values. Otherwise, the reader isn't going to buy in on the scene. Your reader will say, "That's crazy! That Character just wouldn't *do* that."

A Goal Should Be Concrete and Objective

The reader wants to know what it means to win. The reader

wants to know what she's rooting for. A Goal that's concrete and objective is something you could photograph or videotape. Like winning a big race. Or blowing up that bridge before the enemy crosses it. Or popping the question.

SOME EXAMPLE GOALS FOR PROACTIVE SCENES

Now you know the theory of how to define a Goal. Let's look at some examples from the novels we looked at earlier.

Example 1: A Goal for a Proactive Scene in *The Hunger Games*

Chapter 14 of *The Hunger Games* begins with a scene in which Katniss has climbed a tree to escape several of the vicious Career Tributes who want to knock her out of the competition. Katniss has only a knife, while the Careers are well armed with spears, swords, and a bow and arrows. Her situation looks hopeless.

As the scene begins, Katniss spots a nest of tracker jackers.

But what's a tracker jacker? That's not something the reader could know.

A tracker jacker is a mutated form of wasp, and it's part of the Scene Crucible. So Suzanne Collins takes several paragraphs to explain how vicious and deadly tracker jackers are. A few stings will give you terrible hallucinations. A few more will kill you.

You need that information to make sense of Katniss's Goal for this scene.

That Goal is simple. Katniss is going to climb up to the branch holding the nest of tracker jackers and try to saw it off. Carefully, so as not to upset them. Then she'll drop the nest straight down on the Careers and drive them away.

Let's see how good this Goal is:

- Does it fit the time slot for the scene? Yes. It should take only a few minutes to saw off the branch.

- Is it possible for Katniss? Yes. She has a large knife with a serrated edge.
- Is it difficult? Yes. If she vibrates the branch while sawing, the tracker jackers will come out before she can drop the nest—and they'll attack *her*. And she needs to do it during the anthem, when the Careers down below aren't watching her.
- Does it fit Katniss? Yes. Katniss has a Value that nothing is more important than survival. Her Ambition is to stay alive. And her Story Goal is to win the Hunger Games. Attacking the Careers with a nest of hyperpowerful wasps is exactly in line with her Values, her Ambition, and her Story Goal.
- Is it concrete and objective? Yes. Either the wasp nest drops on the Careers or it doesn't.

Example 2: A Goal for a Proactive Scene in *Outlander*

In chapter 12 of *Outlander*, Claire is traveling with a number of Scotsmen to collect rents for the laird. They still have no idea she's a time traveler, but they know she's an Englishwoman and so they don't really trust her. Claire knows they're getting close to the stone circle time portal that brought her to the past, and her Story Goal is to reach that time portal and go home. But she can't get there safely on her own. She's going to need help. In a village named Brockton, Claire and her Scottish friends learn that the English garrison commander from nearby Fort William is in the local inn.

As the scene begins, the leader of the Scots, a man named Dougal MacKenzie, tells Claire that they are going to visit this garrison commander.

Claire immediately forms the Goal for this scene—she wants to persuade the garrison commander, whoever he is, to send her with an armed escort to the stone circle.

Is this a good Goal? Let's check:

- Does it fit the time slot for the scene? Yes. It should take Claire an hour to meet the garrison commander and make her case to him.
- Is it possible for Claire? Yes. She's an Englishwoman. The garrison commander is an Englishman. She just has to cook up some reason why he should give her a few soldiers to take her half a day's journey to the stone circle.
- Is it difficult? Yes. She is not a good liar, and she really has no good reason for being in Scotland. She's tried to lie before and been caught out.
- Does it fit Claire? Yes. She has two Values here. Nothing is more important than staying alive. Nothing is more important than her husband, Frank. Her Ambition is to return home to Frank. Her Story Goal is to find the time portal and pass through it. So asking the garrison commander for an escort to the stone circle is perfectly aligned with her Values, Ambition, and Story Goal.
- Is it concrete and objective? Yes. Either Claire gets a few soldiers and a horse from the garrison commander, or she doesn't.

Example 3: A Goal for a Proactive Scene in *The Godfather*

Chapter 10 of *The Godfather* begins with Michael Corleone looking out the window of the hospital room where his father lies helpless and unguarded. Michael knows that a team of Mafia hit men are on the way to kill his father. Michael has no gun and no allies, but he knows that help will arrive in fifteen minutes, if he can hold off the killers that long.

So Michael's Goal is simple: stall the hit men until help arrives. This Goal is not explicit in the scene, but the reader can easily guess what Michael has in mind, based on what he's thinking and doing. It's obvious that he'll have to out-think his opponents, because he sure can't out-gun them. The reader doesn't know how Michael is going to do that. But Michael doesn't know either. The enormous tension in the scene comes from the fact that Michael is walking into danger unarmed.

Let's check how good Michael's Goal is:

- Does it fit the time slot for the scene? Yes. Michael's brother has told him help will be there in fifteen minutes. That's a fine length for a high-action scene.
- Is it possible for Michael to stall? Yes. We know Michael has seen combat in the Pacific. He's killed people. He won't freak out when he sees a gun. And we know his father and brothers think he's extremely tough.
- Is it difficult? Yes. The enemy will send a driver with three or four armed men. Michael is alone and unarmed. Those are long odds. Michael is a very bright guy, and he's tough. But guns don't care how smart or tough you are.
- Does it fit Michael? Yes. Michael is a Sicilian, and so one of his Values is that nothing is more important than blood relatives. Michael will sacrifice himself to save his father. Of course, this goes against two of his other Values—that nothing is more important than survival, and nothing is more important than being a law-abiding citizen. So Michael's Values are in conflict, and he's consciously making a decision on which one is truly the most important. Michael's Ambition in this novel is going to change. So is his Story Goal. They'll change because his Values were in essential conflict, and very soon he's going to have to choose between them. This scene is his first step on a new path to a new Ambition and a new Story Goal.

- Is Michael's Goal concrete and objective? Yes. Michael's father will be either alive or dead at the end of this scene.

AFTER THE GOAL COMES CONFLICT

We've now looked at the Goals for three example scenes and have found them each to be strong. The Goals have been laid out as quickly as possible, and now the authors will move on to the main body of the scene.

Let's remember that these are Proactive Scenes. Which means they're Goal oriented. The whole purpose of the POV Character in a Proactive Scene is to achieve the Goal in that scene. During the Proactive Scene, your POV Character must never lose sight of that Goal. Everything else in life temporarily has a lower priority than reaching that Goal.

You, the author, should try to set the Goal in your Proactive Scene as quickly as possible and then move directly into Conflict. If you can set the Goal in a sentence, do so. If it takes a paragraph, do so. If it takes more than a few paragraphs, think hard about why you are taking so long to make clear *the most important thing in your POV Character's life at this moment.* Why dither? Get to the point of the scene.

Now that we've learned everything we need to know about Goals, we won't dither either. Let's get to the fun stuff, which is Conflict.

Chapter Eight

HOW TO CREATE A DYNAMITE CONFLICT

As we've said several times, every scene needs to be its own miniature story, complete with a beginning, a middle, and an end. In the last chapter, we saw how the beginning of a Proactive Scene sets the Goal for that scene.

The middle of a Proactive Scene is Conflict, and this will use up the great majority of your word count for the scene.

The Conflict comes directly out of your Scene Crucible. The Conflict may be caused by the environment, by another character, or by the POV Character's own internal conflicting Values. Or any combination of these. All of them can be part of the Scene Crucible.

You'll spend most of your scene showing your POV Character in conflict with her Scene Crucible. If you've been putting off explaining part of the Story Crucible, and you need the reader to understand that part for this scene, now is the time to explain it. Do so as quickly as possible.

HOW MUCH TENSION IN YOUR PROACTIVE SCENES?

The Conflict should be tough on your POV Character. That raises a question. How tough do you want your Conflict to be?

Some novels have ridiculously high-tension Conflict in just about every Proactive Scene. If you're writing an over-the-top action-adventure novel, then that's appropriate and your target audience will accept it. That's the powerful emotional experience they're looking for.

But in most novels, the Conflict is dialed down a bit in some of the Proactive Scenes. Of course some scenes are very high tension, but others are only moderate tension. If you have low-tension scenes, they generally won't be Proactive Scenes; they'll be Reactive Scenes. But more on Reactive Scenes a few chapters down the line.

There isn't any one right answer for what mix of tension you should use for your Proactive Scenes. You should study the category of fiction you're writing, and you should know what range of tension your target audience is expecting. Then write your Conflict in that range.

THE PATTERN FOR CONFLICT

The pattern for Conflict is pretty simple:

- Your POV Character tries something that she expects will take her to her Goal.
- Something or someone tries to block her.
- Repeat this cycle over and over until you're ready to end the scene.

There are no rules for how long this can go on. You might have only one or two rounds of try-something-and-be-blocked. Or you might have five or ten or more. The most important scenes in a book will often go on quite long, stretching out the Conflict and gradually jacking up the tension until it can't go any higher.

SOME EXAMPLE CONFLICTS FOR PROACTIVE SCENES

We've just defined the basic pattern for Conflict in a Proactive Scene. Let's see how that pattern plays out in the scenes we began analyzing in the last chapter.

Example 1: The Conflict for a Proactive Scene in *The Hunger Games*

In the last chapter, we began analyzing a scene in which Katniss is up a tree. Her Goal is to drop a nest of tracker jackers on the Career Tributes on the ground. She wants to do it while the Gamemakers are playing the anthem, which will distract the Careers. Let's see how that works out for her. We'll see the tension rise and fall as the scene progresses. Each bullet point below is one loop of trying-and-hitting-obstacles.

- Katniss moves up higher on the branch she's on. The anthem begins playing, and Katniss begins sawing with her knife. But her hands were burned in the previous scene, and it's agony to grip the knife.
- Katniss keeps sawing through the pain. The anthem ends, and Katniss is only three-quarters of the way through the branch. She has to stop because she can't afford to let the Careers notice what she's doing or they'll pull back to a safe distance.
- Katniss inches back down the branch to her sleeping bag and finds that some wealthy sponsor has parachuted in a gift—ointment for her burns! That's a direct result of her courage, and it gives Katniss a boost.

She puts the ointment on her many burns, and they begin healing. Katniss sleeps through the night. At first light, she goes back to the branch and sees a tracker jacker crawling on the nest. Danger! She ignores her fears and starts sawing. The tracker jackers begin buzzing inside the nest. They're coming out!

- Katniss keeps sawing, faster, faster. A tracker jacker stings her.
- She finishes cutting the branch and shoves it free. The branch with its nest falls to the ground, right in the middle of the sleeping Careers. The nest breaks open. But Katniss is stung twice more.
- The Careers on the ground scatter, with the tracker jackers stinging them fiercely. Two Careers are stung so many times they go down. The others are running for their lives. Katniss climbs down the tree and runs the other way. She's in horrific pain from her three stings.
- Katniss takes out the stingers. She remembers that one of the Career girls had a bow and arrows. She needs that, no matter how dangerous it is to go back. She goes looking and finds the girl, who is just dying. That means the Gamemakers will remove the body shortly, along with the weapons.
- Katniss tears wildly at the bow and arrows. She's already hallucinating. The girl's body is tangled up with the weapons Katniss needs.
- Katniss finally pulls the weapons free. But now she hears somebody coming back to kill her. Peeta arrives first, followed shortly by the biggest thug of all the Careers, a brute named Cato. This can't possibly end well.

Example 2: The Conflict for a Proactive Scene in *Outlander*

In the last chapter, we began looking at a scene in which Claire and her escort Dougal go into the village of Brockton because they've heard the local garrison commander has stayed there in an inn overnight. Claire's Goal is to persuade this commander to give her a few soldiers to take her to the circle of standing stones. She'll need to make up a reason why he should do it. Here's how the scene plays out:

- Claire waits downstairs at the bar while Dougal goes up to the garrison commander's room. Several English soldiers give Claire the eye in a way that makes her feel unsafe.
- Dougal calls Claire to come meet the commander. Claire goes upstairs and finds that the commander is no stranger. He's the evil Captain Randall she met six weeks earlier when she came through the time portal. He recognizes her, and she realizes this is not going to be a cakewalk.
- Claire tells her story of how she came to be here. She's pretending to be a widow from Oxfordshire and claims that her married name is Beauchamp, which was her actual maiden name. (It would be dumb to say that her married name is Randall, which would make her a relative of Captain Randall.) She says she was attacked by outlaws while traveling to meet her dead husband's relatives in France. Her story is full of holes, and Captain Randall isn't fooled. He probes at her story, asking how she can be from Oxfordshire, when no Beauchamps live there.
- Claire asks how he knows, since he's from Sussex. But that's a blunder. Captain Randall never told her where he came from. Her husband, who's a distant descendant of Randall, told her. Randall is instantly suspicious and demands to know how she knows where he's from.

- Claire claims to know from his accent. Randall spars with her a bit on that, trying to catch her in a lie. He tests her knowledge of French, which she passes. Then he asks her maiden name, and Claire has no answer for that, because she's already claimed her maiden name as her married name.
- Claire tries to dodge by asking straight-out to be allowed to continue her journey. Randall glares at her and lays out the case against her, which is devastating. She's obviously lying, and Randall demands to know the truth. He warns her he will take any steps required to learn who she really is.
- Claire asks him what those steps might be. Which turns out to be a mistake.

Example 3: The Conflict for a Proactive Scene in *The Godfather*

In the last chapter, we left Michael Corleone just as he walked out of the hospital onto the street, late at night, alone and unarmed, to wait for a team of Mafia hit men who intend to kill his father. Michael's Goal in this scene is to stall them for fifteen minutes until Corleone Family reinforcements arrive. He's playing a very weak set of cards. Here's how the game unfolds:

- Michael stands under a streetlight so that anyone coming by will see him and recognize him as a Corleone and possibly think he's on guard duty. But the first person to arrive is not the hit men; it's an innocent young baker, Enzo, who is a Family friend, coming to pay his respects to the Godfather. He's a noncombatant, and now Michael needs to get rid of him before the kid gets hurt.
- Michael tells Enzo to leave. He says there may be trouble, and trouble means police. Enzo is not a citizen

and knows he might be deported if there's trouble, but he insists on staying. He'll do what he can to help the Godfather. Michael is stuck with him.

- Michael and Enzo smoke cigarettes, trying to look like foot soldiers of the Godfather. A car comes around the corner and slows down, and the men inside take a long look at Michael and Enzo. The car speeds away, but Michael knows they'll be back, and next time the car will stop.

- Ten long minutes pass, and then three police cars fly in, sirens screaming. Michael thinks they've arrived to help, but two of the cops grab his arms while another one checks him for weapons. The police captain yells at Michael and says he thought he'd cleared out all the hoodlums hanging around, so what's he doing here? One of the cops tells the captain that Michael is the son of Don Corleone.

- Michael demands to know why there are no police detectives up in his father's room to guard him. The police captain flies into a rage and tells him he doesn't care if all the Mafia thugs kill each other. He demands that Michael leave at once.

- Michael realizes that this captain is in the pay of his father's enemy Sollozzo. He calmly says that he can't leave until his father is guarded again. The captain orders one of the cops to arrest him, but the cop points out that they have no grounds. Michael has no weapons, and he's a war hero. There'll be a fuss if they arrest him. The captain says he doesn't care and orders the cop to lock Michael up.

- Michael very calmly provokes the police captain. Knowing that the other cops are not dirty, Michael asks the captain how much Sollozzo is paying him to set up Don Corleone. This pushes the captain over the edge.

ALL GOOD SCENES MUST COME TO AN END

Conflict is good, and in a well-played scene, you'll build up the tension to the maximum level that your Scene Crucible can support. When the tension is maxed out, don't let it plateau. You don't want your reader to get bored. You want your reader to *finish the scene wanting more.*

Break your POV Character out of the Scene Crucible.

When you do that, either the POV Character wins or the Scene Crucible wins.

Those are the only two options. We'll look at those next.

Chapter Nine

HOW TO CREATE A DYNAMITE SETBACK

You're now ready to end your scene. Remember, every scene is a miniature story, with a beginning, a middle, and an end. So the end of your scene must be an *emotionally powerful* ending to this miniature story.

But not necessarily *emotionally satisfying*. Generally, you want the reader to be unsatisfied. You want the reader to be wanting more. You want the reader to turn the page and read the next scene.

And the best way to do that is to end the scene with a Setback. If you can't end with a Setback, then end the scene with a Victory. Do something that closes off the miniature story for your scene, but without closing off the larger story that contains it.

A SETBACK IS RELATIVE TO YOUR PROTAGONIST

There's one point we need to make clear here. What do we mean by a Setback and a Victory?

Remember that your reader is emotionally attached to the protagonist of your main story.

But the lead Character in any particular scene (the POV Character) can be anybody—the protagonist, the love interest, the side-kick, the villain, or some other person.

Everything in your story is measured by your protagonist. When we talk about ending a scene with a Setback, we mean a Setback as measured by the protagonist.

If the POV Character for your scene is working in your protagonist's interests, then a loss for that POV Character is a Setback for your protagonist.

If the POV Character for your scene is working against your protagonist's interests, then a win for that POV Character is a Setback for your protagonist.

And likewise, when we talk about ending a scene with a Victory, we mean a Victory as measured by your protagonist.

BUT A PROTAGONIST CAN BE COMPLICATED

That raises another issue. Your protagonist may not be a nice person. Nobody's perfect, and your protagonist may be flawed.

In *The Hunger Games*, Katniss is a generally likable person, but not entirely. Early on, she gets on our good side by volunteering to replace her little sister in the Hunger Games. That's amazing. That's someone we can root for. But she's got a hard side to her. She's cynical and not a bit romantic. Peeta's in love with her, but she doesn't love him back and she often manipulates him. We're rooting against her there—we don't want the same thing she wants; we want what's best for her. We want her to fall in love with Peeta. So in some scenes, we feel torn. We understand that she wants desperately to survive, and we can get inside her skin and want that too. But at the same time, we want something for her that she doesn't want for herself—we want her to learn how to love.

In *Outlander*, Claire is an entirely likable person. The reader is completely on her side throughout the story. We want her to get home to her husband. But we also feel her growing love for this other man she's met and been forced to marry. Claire is torn and doesn't always know what she wants. And the reader is torn right along with her, because her battle is one good thing against another good thing.

In *The Godfather*, Michael Corleone is a generally likable person who is gradually being pulled over to the dark side. The novel is the story of a good person corrupted. We like Michael. We want what's best for him. As Michael begins to go wrong, we don't want him to go that way. Yet we can also walk inside his skin and understand what makes him turn. We're rooting for him to go straight. But we can't look away as he veers off his original course into a new, dark destiny—as he gradually becomes the new Godfather.

When things get complicated, doesn't that make it even harder to define what we mean by a Victory and a Setback?

We've said that we measure Victory and Setback by the protagonist.

So what happens when the protagonist wants the wrong thing?

We could tie ourselves in semantic knots over this.

But we won't. We'll just define a Victory by what the protagonist wants, even if it's actually bad for him. And we'll define a Setback as what the protagonist doesn't want, even if it's actually good for him.

This means that in some cases, a Setback is good and a Victory is bad.

So be it. Life is complicated.

SOME EXAMPLE SETBACKS FOR PROACTIVE SCENES

Now let's look at our example Proactive Scenes and see how they end. We're aiming for Setbacks here, but sometimes we'll have to settle for Victories.

Example 1: The Victory for a Proactive Scene in *The Hunger Games*

In the last couple of chapters, we've analyzed the Goal and the Conflict for a scene in which Katniss starts out trapped in a tree by several Career Tributes. They mean to kill her, and her Goal is to drop a nest of tracker jackers on them and escape. That turns out to be hard, but she succeeds. All of her tormentors are driven off. It looks like one of them is probably going to die. Katniss sees another that she knows for sure is dying and takes her weapons.

So that counts as a Victory, right? Katniss got what she wanted?

Yes, but Suzanne Collins very wisely turns this Victory on its ear. Two of Katniss's enemies return. The first is Peeta, whom Katniss is convinced is a liar and a murderer.

Katniss tries to shoot him, but the tracker jacker venom has ruined her vision. She can't see well enough to string an arrow.

Peeta has a spear. But he's not trying to kill her. He's screaming at her to run. Katniss still hasn't figured out that Peeta is on her side. She's too befuddled to run. So she stares stupidly at Peeta while he's trying to save her life.

Then Cato appears. Cato is the biggest and baddest of the Careers, and he's demented in his hatred of Katniss. And he's got a sword.

Finally Katniss runs. She can barely see, and she's hallucinating from her stings. But all she can think is that Peeta saved her life.

And she left him alone to face Cato.

So yes, Katniss had a Victory. But with all the tracker jacker venom in her body, the hallucinations, and the guilt of leaving Peeta to face Cato alone, it's a mixed Victory that includes a fair bit of Setback.

As authors everywhere like to say, Suzanne Collins has snatched defeat from the jaws of victory.

And the reader has to turn the page to read the next scene.

Note that the Scene Crucible is now gone. Katniss is no longer in a tree. Two of the Careers who had her surrounded are now dead. There'll be a new Scene Crucible shortly, but it will be different from this one.

Example 2: The Setback for a Proactive Scene in *Outlander*

When we left Claire in the previous chapter, she had just challenged the evil Captain Randall by asking him what he thinks he can do to force her to change her story.

Captain Randall doesn't waste any time. He orders his corporal to stand behind Claire and hold her elbows.

Then he slugs her in the belly as hard as he can.

Claire started this scene hoping to persuade a nice, friendly English officer to help her find her way back to the time portal just a few miles from his garrison.

She ends this scene in massive pain, knowing that this man is not going to help her and he's going to do everything in his power to prevent her from ever reaching that stone circle.

Claire's not going home today, and she may never get home.

And she's going to need some serious protection from this evil man.

That's a Setback.

Once again, the Scene Crucible is finished. Claire will never again be in this room. She'll face Captain Randall again, but in a different place, at a different time, and with different circumstances. And she'll know better what to expect from him. So she'll be better prepared next time.

He'll be better prepared too.

Example 3: The Setback for a Proactive Scene in *The Godfather*

In the previous chapter, we saw Michael Corleone trying to hold off a team of Mafia killers. But he's not prepared for the cops who descend on him and try to clear him away. Michael stands up to them and then asks the crooked police captain how much Sollozzo is paying him to help kill the Godfather.

The captain tells two cops to hold Michael.

Then he punches him in the face, breaking bones and knocking out teeth.

(There are some remarkable similarities between this scene and the one we just looked at in *Outlander*, but they're purely coincidental. The two stories have almost nothing else in common.)

Michael has just had a major Setback. There's a small bit of a Victory mixed in with it. Through the haze of Michael's pain, he sees several cars pull up. Out jump a number of armed men, private detectives hired by the Corleone Family to stand guard over the Godfather in the hospital. A lawyer informs the police captain that the men are fully licensed to carry guns, and if the police captain has a problem with that, he'll be standing in front of a judge in the morning.

So Michael has achieved his Goal for this scene—he's held off the killers until help arrived.

But at tremendous cost. He's just taken an injury that will be with him the rest of his life.

And he's made a powerful enemy in this police captain. The war with the enemies of the Corleone Family is not over.

For Michael, the war is just beginning.

The Scene Crucible has taken a toll on Michael, but it's now finished and we won't see it again. Michael won't be guarding this turf ever again. He won't be his father's sole protector ever again. He will face this police captain again.

But next time, they'll both have a gun.

THE AGONY OF VICTORY, THE THRILL OF SETBACK

In our examples, we've seen one Victory marred by a serious Setback, one full-on Setback, and one Setback sweetened a bit by a Victory.

The Setback in each case is what drives the story forward, forcing the reader to turn the page.

A straight-up Victory would be grounds for the reader to close the book and turn out the lights for the night.

But a Victory mixed with a Setback is a whole different game. It's just as effective as a pure Setback in keeping your reader up far past her bedtime.

And that's a victory for you, the author.

Remember that the purpose of the Setback is to propel the story forward—and force your reader to turn the page to the next scene. So the Setback for your scene should be as short as possible, but no shorter. If you can do it in a sentence, that's great. If it takes a paragraph, that's okay. If it takes a lot of paragraphs, that's less good. Can you do better?

THEN WHAT HAPPENS?

Once you've ended your Proactive Scene, what comes next?

Your reader turns the page because she must know how your POV Character will respond.

You have three terrific options for your next scene:

- Heighten suspense by switching to a new POV Character in the next scene, picking up a different thread of your story. Your reader will continue to worry about the POV Character for this scene you just finished, and that's good. That's an open loop in your reader's brain. You can always continue this thread later.

- Have this same POV Character quickly decide on a new Goal and launch immediately into a new Proactive Scene. This works fine when the next Goal is obvious, or when a new decision can be made quickly. Charge ahead!
- Have this same POV Character spend a bit more time figuring out what to do next. Do this when the next Goal is not obvious and some serious thought needs to go into the next Goal. If you decide to take this route, then you need to know how to write a Reactive Scene. We'll tackle that in the next four chapters.

Part Three

REACTIVE SCENES

Chapter Ten

THE PSYCHOLOGY OF A REACTIVE SCENE

In the last four chapters, we've looked in depth at Proactive Scenes and how they build emotional muscle in a reader—by working the POV Character's emotional muscle harder and harder until that muscle fails.

We're now going to look at Reactive Scenes. They also build emotional muscle, but they do it in a different way—by giving the POV Character time to rest and regenerate.

Both kinds of scenes are necessary.

The context of a Reactive Scene is the Setback of some previous Proactive Scene. The Setback puts pressure on the Character to quit. The Reactive Scene gives your Character a reason not to quit.

Recall that there are three parts to a Reactive Scene:

1. Reaction
2. Dilemma
3. Decision

Let's look at each of these to see why they're necessary.

WHY A REACTIVE SCENE NEEDS A REACTION

When we talk about a Reaction, we mean mostly an emotional reaction. Of course there may be a bit of intellectual reaction ("I can't believe that just happened!") and possibly a bit of physical reaction ("Ouch, my whole body hurts!"), but the emotional part dominates here.

All humans have emotions. When we get hit hard by life, we hurt. Your Character has just been smacked with a major Setback. She's got to be hurting big-time. She needs to take time to feel that pain and work through it. Otherwise, she'll seem inhuman, and your reader won't identify with her.

Your reader wants to step inside your Character's skin. To feel your Character's pain. To empathize. (Unless your reader is a psychopath and can't feel empathy.)

So in the Reaction, you'll punch a lot of emotive buttons in your reader. I can't list them here, because that depends entirely on what the Setback was. The Reaction should show whatever emotions are appropriate to the Setback. They should be at whatever strength is appropriate to the Character. We'll look at some examples in the next chapter.

Eventually, the emotive Reaction will burn itself out. Then it's time to move on, but which way should your Character move?

WHY A REACTIVE SCENE NEEDS A DILEMMA

Your Character now faces a Dilemma. If the Setback in the previous Proactive Scene was a good Setback, *there aren't any good options*.

There are only bad options. The question is which is the least bad option.

That calls for your Character to set aside her emotions and think things out rationally, as best she can. Let's remember that few people ever set aside their emotions completely. There's usually an emotive piece that goes into our reasoning. Marketers know this very well, and a wily marketer will manipulate your emotions into a decision and then give you loads of reasons why that decision is "smart." A wily author may well do the same with her characters.

But your Dilemma will at least appear to be rational. If your Character is Sherlock Holmes, then he'll be mostly rational in his reasoning. (Even Sherlock has emotions.) If your Character is Sonny Corleone, the Godfather's reckless son, he'll be a whole lot less rational. (But even Sonny can follow logic when he's not in a rage.)

No matter who your Character is, *he's going to believe he's being rational* during the Dilemma part of your scene. That's the key. Whether his reasoning is actually sound or unsound, your Character thinks it's solid.

And the whole point of working through the Dilemma is to narrow the options down to one.

WHY A REACTIVE SCENE NEEDS A DECISION

In real life, we often punt on decisions. We decide not to decide. But we know, deep down, that's bogus. That's a bad way to live our lives. We don't admire people who don't make a decision.

We admire people who are decisive.

We want to be decisive.

So we want to watch people being decisive, because it builds emotional muscle memory in ourselves.

Your reader is rooting for your Character to make a Decision. Not a bad Decision—that's not something to admire. And not necessarily a good Decision—that's too much to hope for when your Character is in a tight box.

Your reader is just hoping your Character will make the best Decision possible, given the options.

And your reader doesn't want your Character dillydallying.

Your reader wants your Character to get past her pain, look at her choices, think clearly, make a Decision, and get on with the story.

ADVICE ON REACTIONS, DILEMMAS, AND DECISIONS

Get through the Reaction at a natural speed. That speed depends on who your Character is and how tough the Setback was. Don't be inhumanly quick. Don't wallow too long.

Your Dilemma will take most of the scene. Your Character should consider each option in turn and rule it out, until only one is left. Take as long as you need to do justice to each option, but don't waste time. Your reader is not reading for the intellectual exercise of working through a Dilemma. Your reader is drumming her fingers, waiting for you to get on to the next Proactive Scene.

When your Character has pruned her list of options down to one, that's the Decision. She needs to be sure it's got at least a chance of success. She does not need to know for sure how to make it work—that's for the next scene.

A Decision is not a Decision until your Character commits. Once she commits, the scene is over, and it's on to the next one.

BUT DO YOU REALLY NEED A REACTIVE SCENE?

Reactive Scenes tend to be much lower tension than Proactive Scenes. The modern trend is to use fewer Reactive Scenes. So you have a choice here:

- You may choose to *show* a Reactive Scene as a fully fleshed-out scene.
- You may choose to *tell* a Reactive Scene in a couple of paragraphs of narrative summary.
- You may choose to skip ahead to the next Proactive

Scene, leaving your reader to figure out what happened in the Reactive Scene.

How do you decide? You let the pace of your story guide you.

A Reactive Scene will slow down the pace of your story. If you want a story with an ultra-fast pace, then skimp on the Reactive Scenes. If you want a leisurely pace for your story, then show them all in full.

If you choose not to do a full Reactive Scene, you should still know in your own mind what was the Character's Reaction, what was the Dilemma, what was the Decision, and why that Decision was the best option.

If you choose to do a Reactive Scene, then follow the right order. The Reaction comes first, because emotions trump reason, at least until the emotions burn down. The Dilemma comes second, because reason is slower than emotion. The Decision comes last, because as soon as you have a Decision, the scene is over.

A Decision forces your reader to turn the page to see if the Decision is going to work. The psychology is similar to that for a Proactive Scene. Again, you are creating an open loop in your reader's brain. Will this high-risk Decision work? Or will it only make things worse? Remember that when you create an open loop, your reader can't rest until she closes that loop. Even if it's 3 a.m., your reader needs to turn the page to see what happens next.

Chapter Eleven

HOW TO CREATE A DYNAMITE REACTION

L et's do a quick review.

As we've said a number of times, a scene in your story needs to be its own miniature story, complete with a beginning, a middle, and an end.

The beginning part of a Reactive Scene is the Reaction. Just as with a Proactive Scene, you should identify the POV Character as quickly as possible, preferably in the first sentence. And you should launch into the Reaction as soon as you can.

That raises an obvious question.

HOW DO YOU KNOW WHEN A REACTION IS GOOD?

Part of the reason for having a Reaction is to give your reader a powerful emotional experience. You don't do that merely by naming the emotions your Character is feeling. You want to *show* those emotions. To make your reader *feel* those emotions.

A Reaction Should Show the Character's Emotions

And how do you do that?

We'll see some examples shortly, but the key idea is to show the physical reactions the Character is feeling. Is she crying? Laughing? Blushing? Clenching her fists in rage? Show those things, and you won't have to say that your Character is sad or happy or embarrassed or furious.

There's no standard term used by fiction writers for the process of showing a character's emotions. In my book *Writing Fiction for Dummies*, I adopted the term "Interior Emotion."

There are a zillion techniques for showing Interior Emotion. I can't possibly cover them all here. You could write a whole book on the subject. I covered this a bit in *Writing Fiction for Dummies*, but I strongly recommend Margie Lawson's course *Empowering Characters' Emotions*, which you can buy on her website at www.MargieLawson.com. I also like *The Emotion Thesaurus*, by Angela Ackerman and Becca Puglisi.

A Reaction Should Be in Line with the Character's Personality

Some people just aren't very emotional. Other people seem to always have their emotional meters maxed out.

Different people express their emotions in different ways.

For each of your POV Characters, you need to figure out what their temperament is like and make sure their emotional responses are in line with who they are.

Scarlett O'Hara just isn't going to have the same Reaction as Jack Reacher. Scarlett is very emotional. Reacher isn't. They're both going to feel pain, joy, embarrassment, exhilaration, fear, disgust, and sadness, but they'll do it their own way.

Each of your Characters will do it their own unique way too. Figure out what that is and stick to it.

A Reaction Should Reflect the Character's Values, Ambition, and Story Goal

In chapter 7, we talked about Values, Ambition, and Story Goal. Those things drive your Character. They determine what sort of Goal your POV Character will have in a Proactive Scene. When your POV Character gets smacked with a Setback, those same Values, Ambition, and Story Goal may very well also drive her Reaction. Not always, but sometimes.

A Reaction Should Be Proportional to the Setback

A minor Setback means a minor Reaction. You might be able to get through the Reaction in a sentence, or maybe a paragraph.

A major Setback means a major Reaction. You might need to spend a few pages to work through all the feelings.

My rule of thumb is that a Reaction is like salt—a little goes a long way. The Reaction definitely adds something powerful and good to your story, but there's such a thing as too much of a good thing. So don't get carried away with the Reaction. Work through it and move on before your reader gets tired of the drama.

SOME EXAMPLE REACTIONS FOR REACTIVE SCENES

That's enough theory on how to show a Reaction. In earlier chapters, we've looked at examples of the Goal, Conflict, and Setback/Victory for Proactive Scenes from three major novels. Now let's look at the Reactions from the Reactive Scenes that follow directly after.

Example 1: A Reaction for a Reactive Scene in *The Hunger Games*

Chapter 14 of *The Hunger Games* ended with Katniss escaping Peeta and Cato, carrying her precious bow and arrows. She runs in a blind frenzy until the hallucinations from the tracker jacker venom take over. Then she blacks out.

Chapter 15 begins with her waking up.

There's a paragraph of narrative summary during which time slips by and everything feels all hazy and muddled, as it should when you're coming back slowly to consciousness. Just one paragraph.

Then we go into a couple of pages of Interior Emotion, as Katniss's body slowly returns to normal, enough so she can feel her pain and begin unwinding the emotions she needs to work through.

Her whole body aches. And she's wet all over. And she can barely summon the will to move.

Katniss is so stiff, she wonders how long she's been out. At least a day, she thinks. Maybe longer.

Her whole mouth tastes rotten. Katniss is beginning to return to normal.

She begins flashing back to home, remembering what it was like before the Games, when she dreamed of escaping her dreary life with her friend Gale. But thinking of Gale makes her think of Peeta, who saved her life. Why would he do that? Katniss is beginning to come back to rational thought, but she still can't think why Peeta saved her.

She remembers at last that she has the bow and arrows. She feels excitement over that. Archery is her superpower. She has a chance!

Katniss is actually beginning to feel hope.

And with that, her Reaction is complete. Let's go through our checklist:

- Did the Reaction show Katniss's emotions using the methods of Interior Emotion? Yes, all except the first paragraph.
- Was the Reaction in line with Katniss's personality? Yes. The entire Reaction is vintage Katniss. She feels the pain and then turns rational.

- Was the Reaction in line with her Values, Ambition, and Story Goal? Yes. It begins, as it must, with pain. But soon enough it morphs into the emotions of a survivor. One of her key Values is that nothing is more important than survival. She's not wallowing in her pain. She's moving past her pain to a new hope. She might actually win.
- Was the Reaction proportional to the Setback? Yes. The Setback was huge—she nearly died of the tracker jacker venom. The Reaction is also long—nearly three full pages.

Example 2: A Reaction for a Reactive Scene in *Outlander*

When we left off Claire in *Outlander*, she'd just been slugged in the belly by the sadistic Captain Randall. Her escort, Dougal MacKenzie, goes up to the captain's room and shouts at him while Claire begins to recover.

At first, Claire is mainly feeling physical pain. That eases while she sips a glass of milk.

Then she has to face the psychological pain. Captain Randall looks almost exactly like her husband, Frank. So in her heart, it feels like she's been slugged by a man she's always trusted. That takes longer to go away.

But Claire doesn't yet know how much trouble she's in. Dougal knows, but he doesn't tell her yet. He takes her away from the inn, finds a spring, gives her some water, and tells her a story about Captain Randall.

A few years earlier, Captain Randall ordered two floggings of Claire's friend Jamie Fraser. The first was vicious and nearly killed him. The second was just as bad and came a week later.

Claire lives this story through Dougal's eyes, and it's a brutal story.

This is backstory, but it's essential backstory.

At the end, Dougal tells Claire that Captain Randall has given orders that Claire Beauchamp is to present herself at Fort William on the following Monday.

Claire nearly faints. Rightly so, because now at last she knows what she's up against.

So what's going on? Are there two Reactive Scenes here?

It's a bit complicated, but here's my read on it.

Diana Gabaldon isn't writing these scenes in an exact Proactive Scene/Reactive Scene pattern. She's shuffling the ending of the Proactive Scene together with the beginning of the Reactive Scene.

The Setback from the Proactive Scene is in two parts. The first part of the Setback is the punch, followed by Claire's Reaction to that. Then there's the backstory about Jamie, which is not part of the Setback nor part of the Reaction. It's just backstory. Then comes the second part of the Setback, the order to appear at Fort William, followed by the Reaction to that.

Notice that there's no Dilemma here yet, nor any sign of a Decision. Those will come next.

Once again, we can test these Reactions against our checklist:

- Did the Reactions show Claire's emotions using the methods of Interior Emotion? Yes, a bit. In the first Reaction, we see Claire's hands shaking. We feel her nausea. I think it wouldn't be out of line to show a bit more, but we have several paragraphs. It's enough. In the second Reaction, we see her nearly fainting. In a few short paragraphs, she recovers.
- Was the Reaction in line with Claire's personality? Yes. Claire is relatively tough. She grew up with an archaeologist uncle, living in primitive places, dealing with crises. She can roll with the punches.
- Was the Reaction in line with her Values, Ambition, and Story Goal? Not really, but in this case, it's hard to see

how these could play into her Reaction. She's not really thinking about any of these in her Reaction. They just don't have much role in this particular scene.

- Was the Reaction proportional to the Setback? Mostly. A real punch to the gut would probably take longer to recover from, and there might be permanent physical damage. But it's quite plausible that she'd come close to fainting at the news that she has to face Captain Randall again at the fort in a few days.

Example 3: A Reaction for a Reactive Scene in *The Godfather*

In Michael Corleone's Setback, he has just been punched hard in the face by a corrupt police captain.

Michael's Reaction is written in just a few short paragraphs, but it's extremely powerful.

There's a paragraph telling what he feels when he's punched. It's worth quoting in full here, because it's so short and so precise:

He tried to weave away but the fist caught him high on the cheekbone. A grenade exploded in his skull. His mouth filled with blood and small hard bones that he realized were his teeth. He could feel the side of his head puff up as if it were filling with air. His legs were weightless and he would have fallen if the two policemen had not held him up.

There's a short interlude of a few paragraphs when his father's lawyer arrives with men licensed to carry weapons. The lawyer asks Michael if he wants to press charges against whoever hit him.

Now comes the second half of Michael's Reaction, and it shows us exactly who he is. Michael can barely talk, but he refuses to press charges. He claims he slipped and fell. He's refusing to show pain. He knows the police captain thinks he's weak. Again, this part is worth quoting in full, because it's so sharply focused down to a few dozen words:

He saw the captain give him a triumphant glance and he tried to answer that glance with a smile. At all costs he wanted to hide the delicious icy chilliness that controlled his brain, the surge of wintry cold hatred that pervaded his body. He wanted to give no warning to anyone in this world as to how he felt at this moment. As the Don would not. Then he felt himself carried into the hospital and he lost consciousness.

The two short snippets I quoted above are the heart of Michael's Reaction. How do they rate against our checklist?

- Did the Reactions show Michael's emotions using the methods of Interior Emotion? Yes, absolutely. The reader feels the punch with crystal clarity. And the reader feels Michael's icy rage.
- Was the Reaction in line with Michael's personality? Yes. We've seen hints earlier that Michael is the toughest of the Godfather's three sons, the one most like his father. Now we see the proof. Michael's oldest brother, Sonny, would have fought back in a blind rage, and would have been killed on the spot for attacking a police officer. Michael's other brother, Fredo, would have collapsed, sobbing in helpless grief. Michael reacts like his father, hiding his rage, biding his time, already planning revenge. This is what his family believes is the correct behavior for a Sicilian.
- Was the Reaction in line with Michael's Values,

Ambition, and Story Goal? Yes. Michael has two Values here. Nothing is more important than survival. So he doesn't try for instant revenge that would get him killed. And nothing is more important than honor. Michael's honor has just been violated, and already he's planning how to avenge himself and restore his honor.

- Was the Reaction proportional to the Setback? Yes. Short as the Reaction was, it's incredibly intense.

AFTER THE REACTION COMES DILEMMA

We've now looked at the Reactions for three example scenes. They're executed differently, but they all show a Character responding emotively to a serious Setback.

But there's got to be more to our scene than just a Reaction. The emotive response is only the beginning of the Reactive scene.

How will our Character respond proactively?

We don't know yet.

Our Character doesn't know yet.

That's for him or her to figure out, and it's a serious Dilemma. We'll tackle that next.

Chapter Twelve

HOW TO CREATE A DYNAMITE DILEMMA

After writing the Reaction, you're now well launched. The Reaction was the beginning of the miniature story you're telling in this scene, and now it's time for the long middle.

The middle of a Reactive Scene is a Dilemma. It lays out the current state of the Crucible for your story and begs for a Decision. Not just any Decision. A good Decision. But there apparently aren't any good Decisions handy.

Your POV Character's only task in this scene is to resolve the Dilemma by finding that one good Decision in a haystack of bad ones.

You need to be careful to keep in mind your Character's strengths and weaknesses.

Sherlock Holmes is going to whip through the options flawlessly, rejecting bad idea after bad idea until only one idea remains, the one with the best chance of success.

Huck Finn, on the other hand, won't be that sharp. He's likely to reject a perfectly good plan and go with a bad one, just because he doesn't know any better.

This is a chance to highlight your POV Character's reasoning powers, for better or worse. If you need a not-so-sharp POV

Character to come up with a really clever solution to his current Dilemma, then give him a sidekick for the scene who's quicker on the uptake.

THE PATTERN FOR A DILEMMA

The classic pattern for a Dilemma is pretty simple:

- Your POV Character considers some possible plan for the Goal of the next Proactive Scene.
- She looks at the advantages but then sees that there's a serious hazard in going that way, so she either rejects the idea or puts it on hold.
- Repeat this cycle over and over until you're ready to choose one option.

Notice that the POV Character *doesn't actually act on any of these options*. Not yet. This is not a time for action. This is a time for a well-considered strategic planning session.

You can have her consider as many options as you like. Sometimes there will be only two. Sometimes there will be several.

While there may be an infinite number of possible options, you don't have an infinite word budget for your scene, so it's fine to lump them together into just a few general courses of action. Pick the one that seems easiest and then figure out why it's bad. Then the next, and the next, until you've worked through them all.

So that's the classic pattern.

But you don't always need to use the classic pattern. There are other ways to play a Dilemma. Here are two:

- Sometimes your POV Character doesn't do the heavy lifting on the Dilemma. You may have some other character in the scene who has already worked through the Dilemma. He can simply tell your POV Character what the Decision must be. Then your POV Character spends the scene arguing against that horrible, awful, stupid Decision. Arguing and failing, because in the end, it's clear that it really is the best Decision.

- Sometimes, your POV Character will appear to be doing anything but thinking about her Dilemma. But she is. Not all thinking is conscious thinking. When your body works, your subconscious mind works too. In my day job, I've worked for many years as a computational physicist. I've solved a lot of gnarly problems by going for a walk or mowing the lawn or chopping wood.

In our examples, we'll see all three of these in action. We'll see Katniss work out her Dilemma through physical effort. We'll see Claire have her solution handed to her so she can rail at its colossal stupidity. And we'll see Michael work through his Dilemma with ice-cold logic.

WHAT IF YOUR DILEMMA IS WEAK?

If your POV Character's choice of action seems obvious and clear, then you may not even need a Reactive Scene at all. No Dilemma, no need for a Reactive Scene.

But if you've got no Dilemma, then it may be that the Setback in the previous Proactive Scene wasn't strong enough. Have you shortchanged your reader by not boxing in your POV Character enough? Should you backtrack one scene and make that Setback tougher?

This is a judgment call, and there is no one-size-fits-all answer I can give you. If you feel that a strong Reactive Scene is called for here, then the only way to strengthen the Dilemma is to strengthen the Setback in the previous Proactive Scene. But you might also decide to skip a Reactive Scene and move straight to the next Proactive Scene with an "obvious" Decision. It's your call.

Don't prolong a weak Dilemma by letting your POV Character be too dumb to see that the choice really is obvious. That's just a delaying action, and it's sure to annoy your reader. If the Dilemma is weak and you can't see how to make it stronger, don't drag things out. Get on to the Decision quickly.

When you spend pages and pages on the horns of a Dilemma, it needs to be a Dilemma with some serious horns.

WHY BOTHER WITH A DILEMMA, ANYWAY?

A Dilemma slows down your story. Nothing is *happening* during a Dilemma. People are just talking about things they could do.

So why bother with all that?

One big reason is because *Dilemmas show us what your POV Character is*. A really good Dilemma is usually really good because it lies on the fault lines of the POV Character—on some deep contradiction in her soul.

As we live through the Character's Dilemma, we see what she's made of. For all her life, maybe she's held two contradictory Values as equally true, without really thinking about the contradiction. But when all the money's on the table, which Value does she hold as "more true"?

Remember what Story does. Story teaches the tribe to survive. Story keeps the tribe alive. Story shows the tribe how to thrive. It does that by forcing Decisions and then watching where those lead.

A right Decision gives Story a chance to show the tribe why it's a right Decision.

A wrong Decision gives Story a chance to show the tribe why it's a wrong Decision.

That doesn't mean right Decisions are easy. They're hard.

That's why we need Story—to give us the emotional muscle memory to do the hard right and not the easy wrong.

SOME EXAMPLE DILEMMAS FOR REACTIVE SCENES

Now let's look at the Dilemmas posed to our POV Characters in the Reactive Scenes we've been following.

Example 1: A Dilemma for a Reactive Scene in *The Hunger Games*

Katniss has finally come awake after surviving three tracker jacker stings. She's just realized that she has a fighting chance to win, now that she has a bow and arrows. But a fighting chance is not a plan. Katniss needs a plan. What's her plan?

She's not in good condition to make a plan. The tracker jacker venom has sapped her energy, and she's not thinking clearly. She's shuffling along, just surviving.

But her subconscious is thinking. We can't see it, but we can see her slowly coming back from being nearly dead.

She goes looking for water and purifies some and washes herself off. She treats her burns. She shoots a wild bird and starts cooking it over a low fire.

When she hears a sound, she whirls and discovers she's not alone. The very smallest tribute, a twelve-year-old girl named Rue, is watching her. Katniss could easily kill Rue, but instead she offers an alliance.

Rue is thunderstruck. Everybody else thinks she's worthless. But Katniss sees value in her. Katniss thinks Rue can be a helpful ally against the Careers.

Rue has some herbs that heal tracker jacker venom. She puts some on Katniss's stings, and Katniss instantly feels better. Katniss has ointment, and she uses it to treat Rue's burns. Already, the alliance is paying off.

Katniss has fresh meat and Rue has edible roots and berries, and they make a meal together. They talk.

Rue tells Katniss that the "sunglasses" she found in her pack are night-vision goggles. And she tells Katniss that Peeta isn't just pretending to be in love with her. Peeta is for real.

Then Rue says the crucial thing that Katniss needs to make a Decision. She tells Katniss that the Careers have a camp by the lake with a huge stash of food. They need that stash because, unlike Katniss and Rue, they can't live off the land. If the Careers run out of food, they can't last long.

And in a rush of insight, Katniss finds the Decision she's been looking for. The chapter ends without the reader knowing the plan. But the reader knows Katniss has a plan.

So let's analyze this Dilemma. What happens to bridge the gap between the Reaction and the Decision?

What happens is that Katniss teams up with somebody who has knowledge she doesn't. The two girls ally themselves against the Careers. They pool their medicine. They pool their food. They pool their knowledge.

And they violate the entire spirit of the Hunger Games.

The point of the Hunger Games is to always keep the districts at each other's throats. To destroy trust. To keep them from banding together against the Capitol.

Sure, the Career Tributes make alliances so they can thin the herd a bit. But the Careers never make friends with other Careers. They're always temporary allies.

Katniss and Rue are not just allies. They're friends.

Katniss has been wrestling the entire novel with two Values. Nothing is more important than family. Nothing is more important than survival.

Rue is not part of Katniss's family, but she reminds Katniss of her sister, Prim. Rue is human and she's good, and Katniss effectively makes her family.

Katniss knows that she and Rue can't both survive.

But she puts that out of her head and does the decent thing.

The human thing.

The thing that's kept humanity alive for many ten thousand years.

She forms a community with a stranger.

And by doing that, she comes to a plan that she could not have formed on her own. She needed Rue to reach it. She needed what Rue had and what Rue knew.

At the very end of the chapter, Katniss has a plan. She's made a Decision. We don't know what it is, but we'll find out when we turn the page.

Example 2: A Dilemma for a Reactive Scene in *Outlander*

Claire has just suffered through a double Setback—getting punched in the belly by Captain Randall and then learning that he wants her to report to him at Fort William on Monday. What's she going to do?

Claire is well and truly boxed in. If she reports to the captain on Monday, she could end up in an English prison where she'll rot forever. If she tries to run, her Scottish escort Dougal and his men will chase her down. If she tries to persuade them to help her run away, she's asking them to flout the English for her, an outlander.

And there's the beginning of the solution to Claire's problem.

Claire is an Englishwoman, subject to English law, under the command of the English army. But she's living in Scotland, and Scots are not subject to English law, as long as they're not criminals.

Claire needs to become a Scot.

The only way to become a Scot is to marry a Scot.

Claire doesn't see any of this. There's no way she could know the rules of the game. She's from 1946, and this is 1743.

But Dougal MacKenzie knows the rules, and he's been thinking about Claire's problem for weeks now.

Dougal has another problem. Jamie Fraser is his nephew, a bold young man, charismatic, popular, a brilliant warrior. Jamie is also a political threat to Dougal and his brother Colum, the laird of the castle where Jamie lives. Dougal and Colum know that Jamie might well try to outmaneuver them for control of the clan someday. But if Jamie were married to an outlander, that would mark him forever as a man not to be fully trusted. It would make him just a wee bit of an outsider to the clan.

Dougal and Colum want Jamie to marry Claire. That will solve their problem of Jamie being their political rival. And it will solve Claire's problem with Captain Randall.

That's the Decision Dougal wants to impose on Claire.

He explains the matter to her.

Claire is not pleased with this Decision and says flat out she can't.

What she means is that she's married to Frank Randall, a man of the twentieth century, a man not even born yet. But that's not something she can explain. Nobody knows she's from the future.

So when Dougal asks why she can't marry and asks her point-blank if her husband is still alive, she has to say no.

Then Dougal lays it all out for her. She must become a Scot. That's the only way he can refuse to deliver her over to Captain Randall on the coming Monday.

Unless she wants to go sit in an English prison. But Dougal has laid the groundwork well by telling her in brutal detail about the two floggings Captain Randall ordered for Jamie.

It's a character reference for Captain Randall—he's pure evil.

It's also a character reference for Jamie—he's tough.

If Claire marries Jamie, he'll protect her to the end of his strength.

Claire actually likes Jamie. He's educated and kind and honest. And wildly sexy. It's true he's a few years younger than Claire, but that's not a major difference.

The fact is, Claire still wants to get back to 1946. The way to get there is through the standing stones. Jamie could take her there.

After thinking about it for a while, Claire realizes that she really hasn't got any other options. Feeling her resistance crumbling, she demands to talk to Jamie. He's being forced to marry her, so he ought to have some say in it, right?

But Jamie is quite fine with marrying her.

As a last resort, Claire asks Jamie if it bothers him that she's not a virgin.

Jamie just grins and shrugs and says it doesn't bother him, as long as it doesn't bother her that he is.

Claire is caught massively off guard. She knows Jamie spent two years in the French army. How in the world is he still a virgin? She can't think what to say. She doesn't say a thing.

And having fired her last, feeble shot, Claire has run out of options.

So let's analyze this Dilemma. This is a fine example of a case where the POV Character can't work through the Dilemma on her own. Claire doesn't know enough about English and Scottish law to see that this is the only way. Nor does she have the power to force Jamie to marry her.

So Dougal plays the role of the mentor here, walking Claire through the Dilemma, guiding her toward the solution. This is not something Dougal cooked up on his own, on the spot. His brother Colum is cleverer and put the idea in his head weeks earlier. Dougal is simply executing Colum's plan at the opportune moment.

And it works because Claire has no good choice.

Jamie has a choice. He could say no, and Dougal could marry Claire off to one of the other men. But Jamie knows something nobody else imagines.

Jamie is in love with Claire.

Wildly, madly, insanely in love with her.

He has been practically since he's known her.

Jamie is not being pushed into this marriage.

He's jumping of his own free will.

Claire is being forced to marry, but she won't be sorry.

Example 3: A Dilemma for a Reactive Scene in *The Godfather*

Michael Corleone has just been viciously sucker punched by a corrupt police captain. Michael doesn't fight back, which would get him killed. He doesn't try to press charges, which would put the responsibility for vengeance on the legal beagles.

Michael is taking the load for vengeance onto his own shoulders. But knowing you want vengeance is not the same as knowing how you're going to get it. How will Michael pay back the bad cop?

Michael can't do anything just yet, because he's unconscious in the hospital. But in the morning, he's woken by his father's *consigliori*, Tom Hagen. Hagen takes him back to the well-guarded Family house and brings him up to speed on the way.

Fact 1: The cop who slugged Michael is definitely crooked, definitely in the pay of Sollozzo, who ordered the hit on Don Corleone. The cop's name is Captain McCluskey.

Fact 2: The Corleone Family has just gunned down Bruno Tattaglia, a member of the Family sponsoring Sollozzo. That's payback for shooting Don Corleone. And it's the beginning of what will be a long war between the rival Families.

Fact 3: Don Corleone's right-hand man, a brutal killer named Luca Brasi, is dead—killed the night before Don Corleone was shot. Luca was the Corleone Family's ace in the hole, and now he's gone.

Fact 4: Sollozzo has asked for a meeting, and the only Corleone he trusts is Michael. He guarantees Michael's safety, and he's offering a deal that he claims is so good the Corleones won't be able to resist it. He claims that things are even, now that his ally Bruno Tattaglia is dead. Blood for blood. He wants everyone to declare bygones to be bygones, to move forward without a bloody war.

When Michael gets home, he finds himself in a council of war with his violent older brother, Sonny, his father's *consigliori*, Hagen, and his father's two chief lieutenants.

The question is how to respond to Sollozzo.

This is a serious Dilemma, because Sollozzo put the hit on Don Corleone. Now he claims he wants peace? Can he be trusted? On the other hand, can the Family afford to fight him? Or should they play a waiting game and send Michael to the meeting while they retrench for an all-out war? But doesn't that just buy time for Sollozzo to try another hit on the old man?

The purpose of the meeting is to work through the Dilemma.

Tom Hagen begins by saying that the Family should at least listen to the deal Sollozzo is offering. Because, why not? It might be good.

Sonny is furious. No meeting. No truce. He proposes an ultimatum. The Family should demand Sollozzo's head, or else it's war with his sponsors, the Tattaglia Family.

But that's a terrible idea, and Hagen immediately explains why. Sollozzo is paying off Captain McCluskey, who's acting as his bodyguard. There is no way to kill Sollozzo without going through McCluskey. And killing a New York cop is the surest way to destroy the Family business. The whole city would come down on the Corleones in righteous rage. Sonny's idea is a nonstarter.

Michael asks if it's possible to bring his father home from the hospital. He needs to be in a safe place as soon as possible. If they bring him home, they buy some time. As long as Don Corleone is in the hospital, he's vulnerable to Sollozzo and McCluskey.

But that won't work either. Sonny explains that their father is too badly damaged to be moved. The doctors say moving him would kill him.

Michael now points out that they must kill Sollozzo. Sollozzo can't be trusted. He'll try again to kill Don Corleone, and next time he might succeed. This is not an option. *Sollozzo must be killed right now.*

The others see the logic. But this is not yet a Decision. It'll be a Decision when the group decides who will kill Sollozzo and when and how.

It's a start. But the Dilemma is still staring at them.

Sonny points out the problem with killing Sollozzo—he's guarded by Captain McCluskey.

Michael says that if Sollozzo has to be killed, then McCluskey has to be killed too. Yes, it's extreme. But McCluskey is crooked, and when the city finds out their dead cop was on the Mafia payroll, all their righteous rage is going to fade like smoke. Nobody likes a crooked cop.

But this is still not a Decision.

Who's going to kill Sollozzo and McCluskey?

Michael is now clearly in charge of the meeting. He says that Sollozzo has already asked for a meeting with him, Michael Corleone, Sonny's soft kid brother, the straight-arrow Marine, the Ivy League college boy, the outsider inside the Corleone Family.

So—Michael asks—what if he goes to the meeting? Without a gun, of course. They'll frisk him for weapons. He'll be clean. But the Family will find a way to get a gun to him inside the meeting. Then he'll shoot Sollozzo and McCluskey. How about that?

Sonny tries to laugh him off. That's a stupid idea. If he kills a New York cop, he's going to the electric chair. And anyway, doesn't he know this isn't long-distance, like in a war? When you knock off a Mafia hood, you put a gun to his head and fire and you get blood and guts on your nice suit. Sonny laughs and laughs.

But Michael isn't laughing. Michael is serious. Michael sees that everyone thinks he's soft, and that's his unfair advantage.

Because Michael isn't soft. Michael has guts. Michael was the only son who could ever stand up to the old man. Michael has a part deep inside his soul that's made of ice-cold steel.

It's just logic. Sollozzo must be killed. Therefore, McCluskey must be killed. Michael can do the job because their enemies think he's soft. Nobody else can get close enough to make the hit. It's the only possible solution, and Michael is volunteering. He's got no wife or kids, so if he needs to run and hide for ten years, nothing is stopping him.

From the point of view of the Family, it really is the only solution.

Now let's analyze this process. They work through the Dilemma like it's a problem in logic. Can we try this option? No, because here's why. What about this one? No, here's why. In the end, only one option is left.

It's risky.

It's desperate.

But it's the only option that fits within the Goals, Ambitions, and Values of the men in the room. You may very well argue that this is a terrible Decision, because it doesn't match your life Goal, Ambition, and Values. It doesn't fit with mine either. *The Godfather* is not a story about nice people.

You don't have to agree with the characters in *The Godfather*.

But once you understand their Goals, Ambitions, and Values, you can understand them. You can even feel empathy for them.

You can follow them on this journey down a road you, personally, would never take.

Michael has two Values that are contradictory. Nothing is more important than doing right. Nothing is more important than family. Up till now in the story, he's been living by the Value about doing right. But now he switches gears. The survival of his family was never on the line before.

Now it is, and Michael's true Value emerges. From now on, nothing is more important than family. The Corleone Family.

And this is the solution to a problem that's been looming since the first chapter. Don Corleone is getting old. His first son, Sonny, is too much the bully to be a good successor. His second son, Fredo, is too weak. His third son, Michael, is too honest.

When the Godfather retires or dies, who will be the next Godfather?

With Michael's Decision, we have a possible answer.

AN END IMPLIES A NEW BEGINNING

When the Dilemma ends, we have a Decision, which will launch us into the next scene. (Or into some scene a little further down the road, if you're weaving together several threads in your story.)

Dilemmas tend to be long, whereas Decisions tend to be short.

In the next chapter, we'll look at how you wrap up the Decision in a nice package to finish out your Reactive Scene.

It's not complicated, but you do need to do it right. We'll look at that next.

Chapter Thirteen

HOW TO CREATE A DYNAMITE DECISION

Y ou've now written most of your Reactive Scene. Your Dilemma consumed most of the word count for the scene, and now it's time to end the scene. You do that by choosing one of the options from the Dilemma and making a commitment to it.

WHAT MAKES A GOOD DECISION?

Let's be clear that *your POV Character usually doesn't have any good options.* She has bad options and less bad options. So when we talk about a "good Decision," we're not talking about what's good for your Character. We're talking about what's good for your story.

I don't want to saddle you with a bunch of ironclad rules, because fiction isn't paint-by-numbers. But here are some rules of thumb that will guide you in deciding whether your Decision is strong—one that will give your reader a powerful emotional experience:

- The Chess Principle applies here. When you make a forcing move in chess, it reduces your opponent's options and makes him easier to predict. It's the same in fiction. When your Character makes a bold, assertive move, that gives her an edge over the other people in the story.

- The Decision will be the Goal for some future Proactive Scene, so it needs to be a good Goal as measured by the principles we set out in chapter 7. To summarize, that Goal will need to fit the time slot for the coming scene, it must be possible and yet difficult, it must line up with the Character's Story Goal, Ambition, and Values, and it must be concrete and objective.

- The riskier the Decision, the more clearly the Character needs to admit to herself that yes, it is risky, but it's the least bad option. Readers don't respect a Character who walks into danger stupidly. They do respect a Character who walks in knowing the risks and accepting them for some greater good.

- The Decision should be a full commitment. It's not a Decision if your POV Character is dithering around. She needs to go all in on this Decision. If your Character goes all in, then your reader goes all in. If your Character doesn't go all in, your reader may just go to bed.

SOME EXAMPLE DECISIONS FOR REACTIVE SCENES

Now let's look at the Decisions of our POV Characters in the Reactive Scenes we've been following.

Example 1: A Decision for a Reactive Scene in *The Hunger Games*

When we left off Katniss at the end of her chapter, she had come up with a plan. But Suzanne Collins didn't tell us the plan. In the last paragraph of the scene, Katniss says that she has a plan.

She's not going to play defense anymore. Now she's going on offense. And the chapter ends.

This is one way you can conclude a Reactive Scene. Announce that there's a plan and end the chapter.

Another way is to tell the plan.

Whatever you do, don't toy with the reader by having the character dance around the plan. Either tell the plan, or get on to the next scene.

So what is Katniss's plan?

We learn that in the next chapter.

The plan is to destroy the Career Tributes' food supply.

Of course this is risky. The Careers will fight like crazy to protect their food.

But Katniss and Rue have to take it out, or the Careers will simply play a waiting game until the Gamemakers force them all together, and that's an advantage for the Careers.

If Katniss attacks the Careers, the Gamemakers will focus the cameras on her attack, because it makes for good ratings. They'll give her the time to make her play, which is what she needs.

The payoff on this plan will be huge. The Careers don't know how to live off the land. They don't know how to be hungry. In past years, when the Careers lost their food supply, they generally got killed pretty quickly.

So that's the Decision. Is it a good Decision? Let's analyze:

- Is it a forcing move? You bet it is. Katniss is going to massively reduce the options of the Careers with this move—if she succeeds.
- Will the Decision make a good Goal for the next Proactive Scene? Of course. It's possible but difficult; it's concrete and objective.
- Does Katniss admit it's risky? Yes, but she lays out the logic for it. She's going in with both eyes open.
- Is she fully committed? Absolutely. And so is Rue.

It's a good Decision. And now we have a Goal for the next Proactive Scene.

Example 2: A Decision for a Reactive Scene in *Outlander*

When we left off Claire, she was just coming to grips with the Decision that was provided to her by Dougal MacKenzie—she needs to marry Jamie Fraser.

Dougal has his own reasons for wanting Jamie married. But the fact is, it really is the least bad option for Claire. The Dilemma part of the scene has now led her through all the other options.

The Decision in the scene comes when she agrees in her own mind that yes, she's going to marry Jamie.

Of course it's a shock to her. Up to this point in the novel, she's been focused on getting back to 1946. But she'll never live long enough to do that unless she marries Jamie. So she agrees.

Is it a good Decision? Let's analyze:

- Is it a forcing move? Yes. Claire is switching allegiance to become a Scottish citizen. That cuts off Captain Randall's authority at the knees. He's going to have a lot fewer options now.
- Will it make a good Goal for the next Proactive Scene? Oh yeah. There are some legal issues to resolve. There is the matter of finding Claire a dress on short notice. And there's the huge deal looming that she can't ignore—this won't be a legal marriage unless she consummates it. Claire isn't in love with Jamie, but she can't weasel out of this. She's got to get in bed with Jamie and do the deed. And she likes him enough to know this is going to split her feelings.
- Does Claire admit the risks to herself? The risks here aren't physical. They're emotional. In her own mind, she'll be married to two men, even though one of them

doesn't exist yet. So yes, she feels that this is crazy and is going to rip her heart apart. But she also knows it's necessary.

- Is she committing to this plan? Yes. She's signing her name on the line. She's taking vows. She's getting into that marriage bed. That's some serious commitment.

Claire has some challenges ahead of her in the next scene.

And there's no possible way the reader is going to put the book down here.

That's a good Decision.

Example 3: A Decision for a Reactive Scene in *The Godfather*

When we left Michael, he had just proposed that he meet with Sollozzo and Captain McCluskey and shoot them both.

But it's not a Decision yet. This is a Family council, and it can't be a Decision until the other men agree.

Michael has explained why somebody needs to do it.

He's explained why he's the only person who can get close enough to do it.

The other men sit thinking about that for a minute.

Now comes the Decision. Since it's a group Decision, it has to come in stages, one by one.

Michael's brother Sonny gives him a hug and says he likes the idea.

The Family *consigliori*, Tom Hagen, says he likes the idea, but does it have to be Michael?

They go through all the options again. There is nobody else whom Sollozzo will trust who has the guts to do the job. It really has to be Michael.

But there are some details to work out. How could it be done? They'll get a gun, the coldest one they ever owned. A short barrel, plenty of blasting power, and no need for it to be accurate because the range will be point-blank. They'll tape the barrel and trigger with special tape so it won't take fingerprints. They tell Michael that as soon as he's killed the men, he has to drop the gun and walk away, so he won't be caught with the murder weapon on him. They can deal with witnesses, but not with a smoking gun in his hand. And they warn Michael not to give his girlfriend one hint of what he's about to do.

And that's that.

The Decision is made.

Is it a good Decision?

As we talked about in the last chapter, you don't have to agree with this Decision. You may well say that this is a Decision you, personally, would never make.

But you aren't Michael Corleone.

This is his Decision to make, not yours.

You don't have to agree with it. You just have to understand it.

So let's analyze this Decision based on our criteria:

- Is it a forcing move? Yes, this is checkmate—if it succeeds. This decapitates the opposition. This defeats the Tattaglia Family in one shot. There will be no war because the king, Sollozzo, will be dead.
- Will it make a good Goal for the next Proactive Scene? Yes, it's a dynamite Goal. It's possible, but very, very difficult. It fits one of Michael's Values. It is concrete and objective—at the end of the coming Proactive Scene, either Sollozzo and McCluskey will be dead or they won't be. There's no middle ground here.
- Does Michael know the risks? Absolutely. He knows he could be killed. He knows his best-case scenario is that he'll go on the run for a very long time. Michael is no wide-eyed dummy. But he's dead certain that if he doesn't do this job, his father will be murdered. Desperate times, desperate measures.

- Is Michael committing? You better believe he's committing. He's got to pull the trigger or die trying. There's no third option if he gets cold feet. He's all in on this play.

Michael has a big scene coming up. The biggest he's ever played.

If you can put the book down without watching the next scene, you have no soul.

From the viewpoint of creating a great story, that's a great Decision.

Even though it's a Decision that will cost Michael his soul.

THEN WHAT HAPPENS?

Once you've ended your Reactive Scene, what do you do next?

Your reader turns the page because she must know how this Decision is going to work out.

You have two options:

- Switch to a new POV Character in the next scene, moving to a different thread of your story. Your reader is going to go nuts worrying about the Decision that was just made. Why would you do this? Because it leaves an open loop in your reader's brain to torture her. Of course, you'll pick up this thread later. But in the meantime, those open loops keep the reader turning pages.
- Have this same POV Character launch into a Proactive Scene, in which the Goal is exactly the Decision she just made in this Reactive Scene.

We've now spent four chapters each on Proactive Scenes and on Reactive Scenes. You are well equipped to design any new scene before you write it. You can have quite a lot of confidence that you'll write a dynamite scene that will keep your reader reading until the wee hours.

But what about scenes you've already written? What if they're not quite up to snuff, because you didn't know how to design them when you first wrote them? Or what if you knew how to design a good scene, but you didn't actually bother to do the design work up front, and now you've got a scene that isn't your best work?

Can you turn a sow's ear into a silk purse?

Yes.

No.

Maybe.

Read on.

Part Four

WRAPPING UP

Chapter Fourteen

TRIAGE—HOW TO FIX YOUR BROKEN SCENES

U p till now, we've been talking about the ninth step in the Snowflake Method, the step where you *design each scene before you write it.*

Now we're going to talk about *editing your scene after you write it.*

So now we're talking about the second draft of your story.

You'll probably make major changes to many of the scenes in your second draft. There are several reasons why any given scene might need fixing:

- You might not have designed your scene before you wrote it, and therefore it might have no design or a bad design.
- Even if you designed your scene before you wrote it, your design might have been off a bit. Sometimes you can't tell it's an off design until you write it.
- Even if your design was terrific, the scene might have evolved while you wrote it, and it might have ended up having a different design than you intended.
- Even if you designed and executed the scene perfectly,

you might discover that your main story needs tweaking, and this scene is now going to have to change to fit the main story.

All writers are human, and most writers find that a lot of their scenes need serious work on the second draft. There's absolutely nothing wrong with that. Often the only way to get to a perfect final draft is through a really terrible first draft. Most professional writers will tell you they've written a lot of bad first drafts. I certainly have. No shame in that.

So what do you do about it?

TRIAGE—CHOOSING YES, NO, OR MAYBE

On the battlefield, medics make triage decisions all the time:

- This person is going to live, even if I do nothing for him.
- This person is going to die, no matter how much I do for him.
- This person's life is in the balance, and *I need to treat him right now.*

Triage is important. The medic probably has far too many patients and nowhere near enough time. He may also be under fire from the enemy. It's critical to not waste time on patients who are definitely going to live or definitely going to die. The medic needs to put all his resources into the "maybe" patients—the ones he can make a difference on right now.

Triage works the same way when you're editing scenes in your second draft. There are three decisions you can make:

- Yes, this scene is fine as it is. It may need minor tweaks in the later drafts, but the design is strong and I executed the design well. I'll mark this scene Yes and move on to the next one.

- No, this scene is terrible, and there is no possible way to make it better. It won't help to fix the spelling or to put commas in the right places or even to juice up the action. The scene itself just doesn't work and never will. I'll mark this scene No, because I need to junk this scene. Either I'll design a whole new scene and then write it, or else I won't replace this scene with anything.
- Maybe this scene can be saved, but it's going to need a redesign and a rewrite. And I'll do that right now.

So those are your three possible decisions. How do you know which is right?

HOW TO DECIDE ON A YES

I have two requirements to give a scene a passing grade. The scene usually has to pass both of these tests:

- The scene works as a miniature story in its own right. When I get to the end of the scene, it has given me a powerful emotional experience.
- I can identify the Crucible for this scene. For a Proactive Scene, the Crucible is whatever is causing the Conflict. For a Reactive Scene, the Crucible is the specific Dilemma.

If a scene passes both of the above requirements, then it gets a Yes.

If it doesn't, I have to come up with a very strong and compelling reason why this scene should get a pass. That can happen. Writing fiction is not about following a mindless set of rules. There can be a reason to accept a scene that doesn't pass my tests.

I want to know that reason.

In every second draft, a few scenes actually pass.

But a few also fail.

HOW TO DECIDE ON A NO

I don't like to fail a scene, because it took some hard work to write it in the first place, and I'd like to salvage that if I can. But here are some reasons why I'll fail a scene:

- The scene no longer fits the larger story that I'm telling. If the scene doesn't fit, it doesn't fit. Junk it.
- The scene doesn't give me a powerful emotional experience, and I can't see how I ever imagined it could. Really, the whole scene is terribly misconceived. I must have been under the influence of some very bad chemicals when I wrote it, because it has no oomph and it never will.
- The scene has no identifiable Crucible, and I can't see any reason to think that a Crucible can now be welded onto it.
- The scene is not a story and never will be a story, no matter what I do to it.

Every scene has to pull its own weight. Every scene must be a story. Every scene must give the reader a powerful emotional experience. If a scene is doing nothing more than "setting the stage," then it's a failure. If a scene is doing nothing more than "filling in the backstory," then it's a failure. If a scene is doing nothing more than "showing character motivation," then it's a failure.

All of those are good things. Many scenes will set the stage and fill in backstory and show character motivation. But they need to be doing more. They need to be telling a story. They need to be showing the reader a movie in her head.

If your scene is not pulling its weight and can't ever pull its weight, then slit its throat, because it's sucking the life out of your story. Show no mercy. Throw its body to the sharks. Walk away.

But kill it the right way.

You might still be able to sell it for parts.

When I decide to kill a scene, I don't actually delete it.

I might change my mind. Or I might want to salvage some of the dialogue. Or a lot of things.

I mark it for future deletion and move on.

Then in the next draft, I'll delete all scenes that I marked for deletion in this draft. (When I start a new draft, the first thing I do is make a fresh copy of the manuscript document and rename it with "Draft 2" or "Draft 3," etc., as part of the name. Then I work on the new draft, and I never change the previous draft again.)

That way, if there's one good sentence or phrase or bit of dialogue that I might want in a future draft, I'll always have it.

I have killed many scenes in my life, always with a clear conscience.

But the great majority of scenes don't need killing.

They need healing.

WHAT TO DO WITH THE "MAYBE" SCENES

Most of my scenes get marked Maybe. If they aren't a definite Yes and they aren't a definite No, then they get a Maybe.

And that means I'm going to do everything I can to make them healthy.

There's a process for doing that. Here it is:

1. Decide what kind of scene this should be. Is it a Proactive Scene or a Reactive Scene? You may have

intended it originally to be one or the other. Is that decision still good? Or did you never decide in the first place? Did you just write the scene without designing it? It's okay if you did a bad design or no design on the first draft. It's not a crime. But now is the time to decide what this scene should be. If you really can't decide, then *mark it for deletion, because this scene can't be saved.*

2. If you decide it's a Proactive Scene, write down what the Goal is, what the Conflict is, and what the Setback or Victory is. I strongly recommend spelling out what the Crucible is.

3. If you decide it's a Reactive Scene, ask yourself whether you can skip this scene altogether. The trend in modern fiction is to have fewer Reactive Scenes. Can you just replace this scene with a few paragraphs of narrative summary? Can you skip even those and go straight to the next Proactive Scene? Or do you definitely need a Reactive Scene here, if only to give your reader a chance to catch her breath?

4. If it's a Reactive Scene and you intend to keep it, write down what the Reaction is, what the Dilemma is, and what the Decision is. Again, I recommend spelling out the Crucible.

5. If possible, write down the powerful emotional experience you expect the reader to have in this scene.

6. Rewrite the scene.

7. You will need to triage the scene again after rewriting it. You can do that right away, or you can mark it to be done later, but you can't assume that the scene now gets a pass just because you rewrote it once. The scene still has to be tested to make sure it works as a story. So triage it again, either now or later.

A lot of work, no?

Of course it's a lot of work. Editing is hard work. Professional writers edit their work, and they edit it hard. Be a professional.

AN EXAMPLE OF SCENE TRIAGE

I don't have the original drafts of *The Hunger Games* or *Outlander* or *The Godfather*. I'd bet the authors did some serious triage on most of their scenes, but I have no way to know what they did. All I can see is the end results.

The only scenes I've seen triaged are my own.

So the only examples of scene triage I can show you are triages I've done on my own books.

The example I'll show you is from my novel *Oxygen*, which I coauthored with my friend John Olson.

Oxygen is a science fiction suspense novel about the first human mission to Mars, set a few years in the future. John and I published the book in 2001, and we set it in a year that was then the future—2014. We worked out the planetary orbits and planned the mission based on the actual positions that Earth and Mars would have in 2014. Liftoff was scheduled for the day before the Super Bowl, with a landing planned for July 4. (In this novel, TV ratings were important to NASA because of funding problems, so they chose dates that would get maximum ad revenue for a US audience.)

The Crucible for *Oxygen* is quite simple. Two months into the mission, an explosion on the *Ares 10* leaves the four astronauts with only enough oxygen for one of them to reach the Red Planet alive. Who decides who will live and who will die? And who enforces that decision?

A technical note: On a spacecraft, oxygen is made by breaking apart water or carbon dioxide using electricity. Our explosion doesn't actually destroy any oxygen. It destroys most of the solar panels that supply electricity. As the ship gets farther from Earth, there is less sunlight and therefore less electricity. We calculated that by April 10, there would not be enough juice to keep the four astronauts alive.

More on the Crucible: Of the four astronauts, two are men and two are women. Bob has a serious crush on Valkerie, but she doesn't know it.

After the explosion, the middle of the novel tells how NASA cooks up an impossible plan to save all four astronauts. To make it work, everything has to go just right:

- The ship doctor, Valkerie, will put the other three astronauts into a temporary coma to conserve oxygen.
- Valkerie will stay conscious and tend to them for several weeks.
- NASA will redirect a robot ship that is also on the way to Mars to do a deep-space rendezvous with the astronauts' ship around May 16. The robot ship was launched a month earlier than the astronauts, so it's on a somewhat different trajectory.
- Just before the rendezvous, Valkerie will bring Bob out of his coma to walk her through the docking procedure with the robot ship.
- They will cannibalize the robot ship's solar panels. That should give their ship enough electrical power to start making oxygen again.

John and I are geeks, and we actually worked out the orbital mechanics, the oxygen requirements, the electrical power supply equations, the dates, everything. We worked really hard. We did a ton of research. And we were extremely proud of ourselves for figuring out a way to save our crew.

But you're probably already laughing at us for being stupid.

Because if our plan worked, the crew would be saved on May 16. Giving them seven more weeks of happy, happy, happy—all the way to Mars.

That's great for the crew.

Terrible for the story.

John and I didn't figure this out until we got to the rendezvous scene.

Then we panicked.

We still had more than a hundred pages of story.

And not much conflict for the rest of the novel. (There was some conflict planned in the synopsis, but when we came to write this scene, we decided it was dorky and contrived, and we didn't think it was enough to carry the story.)

That was a disaster for us.

We had already sold the book.

We had already received the advance.

We had told all our writer friends we were getting our novel published.

And now we had a story that was doomed to fail.

On a long Sunday afternoon, we had a panic meeting by phone. We talked for hours. And we triaged the rendezvous scene.

The original plan was that the scene would be a Proactive Scene, like this:

- Goal: Rendezvous with the robot ship.
- Conflict: The robot ship is coming in a bit fast. Bob has just come out of a coma and is too tired to help much. Valkerie is not a pilot, but with some advice from Bob, she slows down the robot ship just enough.
- Victory: They execute the rendezvous with the robot ship.

When we wrote the proposal, we were absolutely convinced that our crew had to make that rendezvous. Because if they missed, there was just no possible way to keep them alive even a few days longer. Our crew would die if they missed the rendezvous.

We didn't want them to die.

But the rendezvous was ruining the story.

We finally decided that *they had to miss the rendezvous.*

A technical note: A rendezvous requires that the ships must have almost zero relative velocity. You can't slam two ships together at high speed. You gently nudge them together. But in space, you don't have brakes. So you slow down the same way you speed up—by firing your engines. But rocket fuel is heavy, and you only have so much.

So we revised the plan for our scene to this:

- Goal: Rendezvous with the robot ship.
- Conflict: The robot ship is coming in quite fast, more than two hundred meters per second. It fires its burners to slow down, but it doesn't have enough fuel, and it flames out.
- Setback: The robot ship goes whizzing past our crew and rapidly disappears into the blackness of space. Our heroes have missed the rendezvous, and now they're going to die.

That's a much healthier story, right?

Of course, now we had to think really hard. How in the world were we going to save our crew? We didn't want them to die, but there was nothing left on their ship to cannibalize for oxygen, too little electricity to keep making enough oxygen, and no more robot ships to take solar panels from.

But there was one small source of oxygen we hadn't thought of, because it was way too weird. And anyway, it was way too little. And also it was way too risky.

But when you're about to die, nothing is too weird, too little, or too risky.

So our astronauts gave it a shot, and that crazy gambit gave us another hundred pages of story, with all sorts of Goals, Conflicts,

Setbacks, Reactions, Dilemmas, and Decisions along the way. We finished the book and our editor was happy, even though we didn't follow the synopsis we had sold him. Because the new story was better.

Mission accomplished.

SO THAT'S TRIAGE

Test every scene.

Accept the strong.

Fix the weak.

Kill those that are doomed to die.

No exceptions.

CHECKLIST: HOW TO WRITE A DYNAMITE SCENE

This chapter summarizes the high points of every chapter in this book. If you've read this far, you've learned all the details, so these notes are just reminders of what you've learned.

WHAT YOUR READER MOST DESPERATELY WANTS

The one thing your reader most desperately wants is Story. Story is what happens when you walk through great danger in somebody else's skin. Story builds emotional muscle memory. Story works itself deep inside you because it teaches you how to survive while giving you a powerful emotional experience.

A STORY IS A CHARACTER IN A CRUCIBLE

A Character is a person who desperately wants something she can't have. A Crucible is the reason she can't have it. Story delivers a powerful emotional experience to your reader by giving her the illusion that she is the Character in the Crucible you create.

EVERY SCENE IS A MINIATURE STORY

Your story is made up of many scenes. And each scene needs to be a miniature story in its own right, delivering its own powerful emotional experience. Therefore, every scene needs to feature one or more Characters in a miniature Scene Crucible. At the end of the scene, the Scene Crucible is going to break and you won't use it again. But the larger Story Crucible remains to the end of the story.

EVERY SCENE NEEDS A POINT-OF-VIEW CHARACTER

In each scene, you choose one POV Character to be the lead character for that scene. The emotions of that scene are measured by how they affect the POV Character and how they affect the protagonist of your story. You have six options for how to show the POV Character. Choose one:

- First person
- Second person
- Third person
- Third-person objective
- Head-hopping
- Omniscient

You have three choices for how to show the timing of the scene:

- Past tense
- Present tense
- Future tense

EVERY SCENE NEEDS A CRUCIBLE

Every scene needs a Scene Crucible, which will last for exactly that one scene and then will be broken. If you need to explain backstory or your story world to make your Scene Crucible intelligible, then explain it just when you need it. There are two standard shapes for a scene, the Proactive Scene and the Reactive Scene.

A Proactive Scene looks like this:

1. Goal
2. Conflict
3. Setback (or sometimes Victory)

A Reactive Scene looks like this:

1. Reaction
2. Dilemma
3. Decision

The Scene Crucible for a Proactive Scene is whatever might cause your POV Character to fail to achieve her Goal in the scene.

The Scene Crucible for a Reactive Scene is whatever might cause your POV Character to quit the story.

A Scene is broken when you can't say what the Scene Crucible is.

THE PSYCHOLOGY OF A PROACTIVE SCENE

A Proactive Scene punches a number of emotive buttons in your reader. The Goal for a likable POV Character makes you admire her and hope she'll reach her Goal. The Goal for an unlikable POV Character makes you dislike her and hope she won't reach her Goal. The Conflict makes you worry about what's going to happen and keeps you turning pages. The Setback causes you to feel bad for your story's lead Character and forces you to turn the page to see how she'll get out of her troubles. If there's a Victory, you feel good and may decide to close the book at a good stopping place, so it's always good to try to snatch defeat from the jaws of victory.

HOW TO CREATE A DYNAMITE GOAL

A Goal is good when

- It fits the time available for the scene.
- It's possible.
- It's difficult.
- It fits your POV Character.
- It's both concrete and objective.

HOW TO CREATE A DYNAMITE CONFLICT

Conflict can be high tension or low tension; you get to decide what the right mix is for your category of book. Conflict is just a series of attempts by your POV Character to achieve her Goal. Each attempt meets an obstacle, and the tension in the scene rises through the scene. When you run out of obstacles, it's time to end the scene.

HOW TO CREATE A DYNAMITE SETBACK

A Setback is a defeat for the protagonist of your story, not necessarily a defeat for the POV Character in the scene you're writing. If your POV Character is the villain of the story, then when he wins, that's a Setback for your protagonist. You can't always end a scene on a Setback, because sometimes things are so awful that they can't get worse without your POV Character dying. So you sometimes need to end a Proactive Scene with a Victory, but you should try to make it a mixed Victory if you can.

THE PSYCHOLOGY OF A REACTIVE SCENE

A Reactive Scene needs to start with a Reaction, which is mostly emotional. This is your chance to give your reader a powerful emotional experience via empathy with your hurting Character. The Dilemma that follows is not emotional—it's intellectual. This gives your reader a chance to learn how to face a crisis in new ways. The Decision gives your reader the chance to experience decisiveness, which is something we all admire because it's rare.

The trend in modern fiction is to write fewer Reactive Scenes, so it's okay to trim down a Reactive Scene, to tell it in narrative summary, or to skip it altogether.

HOW TO CREATE A DYNAMITE REACTION

A Reaction is good when

- It shows the POV Character's emotions and lets the reader experience those fully.
- It's in line with the POV Character's personality.
- It's in line with the POV Character's Values, Ambition, and Story Goal.
- It's proportional to the Setback.

HOW TO CREATE A DYNAMITE DILEMMA

A Dilemma shows your POV Character considering several possible plans of action, but not yet taking them. The problem is that all options are bad, and your POV Character must figure out which is the least bad option. A Dilemma will sometimes show the POV Character being told what she should do, and then she has to convince herself that she agrees. And sometimes a Dilemma will show a POV Character filling up her time with physical actions while her subconscious mind works out the solution to her problem.

HOW TO CREATE A DYNAMITE DECISION

A Decision is the resolution of the Dilemma. It will not be a good option, but it will be the least bad one. A Decision is strong when

- It's a forcing move—the POV Character decides to do something that will limit her opponent's options.
- It will make a good Goal for some future Proactive Scene.
- If the Decision is risky, then the POV Character admits the risk, which lets the reader continue respecting her.
- It's a firm commitment—the POV Character needs to go all in on this new plan.

TRIAGE—HOW TO FIX YOUR BROKEN SCENES

After you've written your story, you still need to edit it. Part of the editing job is to look at each scene and make a triage decision—yes, no, or maybe.

A few scenes will be so right, you can immediately mark them Yes. Usually, a scene gets a Yes if all of the following are true:

- It's clearly a story in its own right and gives you a powerful emotional experience.
- You can easily say what the Scene Crucible is.

A few scenes will be so wrong, you can immediately mark them No. Usually, a scene gets a No if at least one of the following is true:

- The larger story has changed, and the scene no longer fits it.
- The scene fails to give a powerful emotional experience, and it's obvious that it never will.
- The scene has no identifiable Scene Crucible, and there is no way to cobble one together.
- The scene is not a story and can't be made into a story.

Most scenes will get a Maybe, and then you need to try to redesign them using this procedure:

- Decide whether the scene should be a Proactive Scene or a Reactive Scene. If neither makes sense, mark the scene No for deletion.
- For a Proactive Scene, write down the Goal, Conflict, and Setback (or Victory).
- For a Reactive Scene, ask yourself whether you even need the scene at all. Can you summarize it or delete it without harming the story? Will you improve the pacing of the story by deleting it?
- If you decide to keep the Reactive Scene, write down the Reaction, Dilemma, and Decision.
- Write down the powerful emotional experience you want this scene to give your reader.
- Rewrite the scene.
- Triage the scene again to be sure that it now passes, or else mark the scene to be triaged again later.

When every scene in your story has been triaged and you have only scenes that have passed your test, you're ready to move on to editing your story at a finer level of detail. Every scene in your story is now structured to be a dynamite scene.

WANT TO CONTINUE LEARNING?

Want to learn more about how to write fiction?

Take a look at my best-selling how-to guide, *Writing Fiction for Dummies*. Since its publication in 2009, this book has become one of the standard reference books on fiction writing. Learn how to

- Organize your life and your writing.
- Write your first draft using the creative paradigm geared for you.
- Edit your manuscript to get agents and editors drooling.
- Find an agent and sell your manuscript to a publisher.

IF YOU ENJOYED THIS BOOK...

Word of mouth is the most powerful marketing force in the universe. If you found this book useful, I'd appreciate you rating this book and leaving a review. You don't have to say much—just a few words about how the book made you feel or how it helped you learn something new.

Thank you so much! I appreciate you!

ABOUT THE AUTHOR

Randy Ingermanson is the author of six award-winning novels and two best-selling books on how to write fiction. He has taught at many writing conferences over the years and is well known around the world as "the Snowflake Guy." He runs the **Advanced Fiction Writing** website, and publishes the free monthly **Advanced Fiction Writing E-zine**, a wildly popular e-mail newsletter on fiction writing. He also blogs when the spirit moves him, and he's the creator of **Snowflake Pro**, a software tool that makes the Snowflake Method fast, easy, and fun.

You can read all the unfortunate details about Randy and sign up for his e-zine and blog here:

AdvancedFictionWriting.com

ALSO BY RANDY INGERMANSON

Advanced Fiction Writing Series

1. How to Write a Novel Using the Snowflake Method

2. How to Write a Dynamite Scene Using the Snowflake Method

Writing Fiction for Dummies

Copyright © 2018, Randall Ingermanson
All rights reserved.

First edition, Ingermanson Communications, Inc., 2018,
AdvancedFictionWriting.com
Cover design by Damonza.com, adapted by John B. Olson

ISBN: 978-1-937031-18-3

❀ Created with Vellum

79817391R00086

Made in the USA
San Bernardino, CA
19 June 2018